THE
NO-GOSSIP
ZONE

A NO-NONSENSE GUIDE TO A HEALTHY, HIGH-PERFORMING WORK ENVIRONMENT

SAM
CHAPMAN
WITH BRIDGET SHARKEY

SOURCEBOOKS, INC.®
NAPERVILLE, ILLINOIS

Published by Sourcebooks, Inc.
P.O. Box 4410, Naperville, Illinois 60567-4410
(630) 961-3900
Fax: (630) 961-2168
www.sourcebooks.com

Library of Congress Cataloging-in-Publication Data
Chapman, Sam.
  The no-gossip zone : a no-nonsense guide to a healthy, high-performing work environment / Sam Chapman with Bridget Sharkey. — 1st ed.
    p. cm.
  1. Work environment. 2. Industrial hygiene—Management. 3. Performance. I. Sharkey, Bridget. II. Title.
  HD7261.C43 2009
  658.3'8—dc22
                              2009010283

Printed and bound in the United States of America
BG 10 9 8 7 6 5 4 3 2 1

For Laura and Ben

CONTENTS

ACKNOWLEDGMENTS

Thanks are due to many people in my life for the content in this book. First and foremost, I would like to thank my wife, Laura Berman, for all her love and support always. I learned both publicity and love at her knee and I honor her wisdom and spiritual grace. Secondly, I would like to thank my father for all his guidance and mentoring. My three boys, for whom I live, are too young to read this book but will grow up in a No-Gossip Zone filled with love.

I would like to thank my colleague and coauthor, Bridget Sharkey for being a true partner in this book and in my business life. Bridget gets me in a way that made this all possible. Also, I'd like to thank our other colleagues who chipped in on the work, Michelle Mekky, Kathleen Streit, Andrea Cordts, Lina Khalil, and Amanda Aldinger. And to all the life coaches who changed my world and continue to do so every day, Diana Chapman (no blood relation) and Jim Dethmer and Jack Skeen, thank you for your guidance and inspiration. Diana in particular taught me much of what I write about in this book and guided me through the transition of my life to the No-Gossip Zone. Finally, I would like to thank my wonderful agent, Sharlene Martin of Martin Literary Management, and my editor, Peter Lynch of Sourcebooks, for making this process so enjoyable and for helping to turn this book into a reality.

INTRODUCTION

Communication is the cornerstone of all of our relationships, including our business relationships. The ability to communicate is a must in today's corporate world, yet most people never learn how to do so effectively and successfully. This is because most people do not know how to communicate *authentically*, which means to communicate honestly, fully, and promptly. Once you learn how to communicate authentically and implement these tools in your office, your joy, productivity, and creativity will increase immeasurably and your relationships will improve dramatically.

AUTHENTIC COMMUNICATION

If you are ready to start living an authentic life, both inside and outside the office, you might be wondering where to begin, especially if you are not in a position to make managerial decisions at your job. After all, when you work in a large corporate firm, you might feel that you are powerless or incapable of effecting change on a large level.

That depends on your definition of large. No, you won't be able to make your coworkers positive and proactive, and you won't be able to make your employer committed to an authentic workplace. But even if you were the head mogul at your office, you still wouldn't be able to force people to truly change. All you can do is make changes within yourself, regardless of your position on the totem pole. But the good news is, once you start making these changes, you will notice the ripple effects throughout your life.

If you aren't sure where to begin, start small.

Remove gossip from your work life, and no longer listen to or participate in negative conversation about someone who is not in earshot. Just by making this small step you can transform your work life. Not only will you no longer feel guilty or ashamed after a particularly nasty gabfest, but you will also no longer attract the kind of people who enjoy gossiping and cutting other people down. Think of it as a cleansing process, both for your inside and for your outside. And if you have friendships that you don't want to lose, simply ask your coworkers to please no longer gossip around you. No doubt they will respect this new commitment you have made and will try to follow suit, and not just when they are in your presence.

The next step is to ensure that you own your 100% of every situation, every thought, and every emotion. This means that you no longer blame other people for ruining your day, not meeting deadlines, etc. Take responsibility for your role in the positive and negative occurrences in your life.

For some people, this might even mean looking for a new job. If you truly hate your job and seek a new career path, then sitting around and complaining about it isn't fair to you or the people around you. Own your 100% and commit to a job search and finding a career that you really love.

Or perhaps owning your 100% means you need to take responsibility for the fact that your relationships with your coworkers or employees aren't as healthy as they should be. Maybe you haven't treated the people around you with the respect with which you would want to be treated. Maybe you have gossiped, complained, and whined your office right into a full-blown toxic environment. The good news is that you can turn it all around and become the *good* example that your colleagues follow rather than the bad.

The next important step is to make sure you are living a balanced life. You might not have control over whether or not your boss calls you late at night, or whether or not you have to work all weekend to please a client. But you do have control over whether or not you plan to commit to an office and a career that take so much time away from your personal life and your family.

If you don't choose to make your job your life, speak to your employer about how you can make your workload more balanced. Lay out the reasons why your time away from work is so precious to you (you need to relax, see your children, exercise, recharge your batteries, etc.), and then ask if there is a solution that will work for both you and the company. Then make sure you are getting the most out of this time off. Turn off your phone, shut off your work email, and be present with your family and friends.

By following these three simple steps, you can begin to implement a basic plan for authentic communication in your life. Then, chapter by chapter, you can take on the more complex ideas until you have mastered a life of majesty, grace, and presence.

MY EXPERIENCE: HOW AN EMPLOYER CAN FOSTER A HEALTHY WORK LIFE

When I first implemented a No-Gossip Zone in my office, I wasn't aware of how the idea would spread. What began as a quiet little office agreement soon became fodder for national and local media, and as a result I realized that our policies at Empower Public Relations were quite noteworthy.

In fact, the No-Gossip Zone was received so well, the media contacted me for other corporate-culture advice. Among other policies I shared were our no BlackBerrys after 6:00 p.m. rule and our free lunch program. When other corporations started following suit, I knew we had an audience for what was happening in our office. That's when I decided to write this book.

Just a few years ago, I was a typical businessman in corporate America. I was a venture capitalist who financed start-up companies and led them to success. I schmoozed, I raised funds, and I worked late, burning the candle at both ends. I went home every night physically exhausted and emotionally drained. My bank account told me I was very successful, but my body and my mind told me something different.

Thankfully, I didn't have to shy from my destiny for very long. I often accompanied my wife—the nation's leading sex therapist, Dr. Laura Berman—to her television appearances and radio shows, and as a result I became well acquainted with the backstage prepping that takes place. And I discovered that I had quite a knack for it! From coming up with titillating topics to brainstorming funny and sexy talking points, I soon realized that I loved working with the media—and that they loved working with me, if I do say so myself!

I took my love of working with the media and funneled it into my new business, Empower Public Relations. Empower PR is creative-driven and built around pitching the media regarding what is interesting and sexy about each client. We discover what makes a client interesting to the media and then teach the client how to subtly mention (called "bridging") their business message during a television segment or interview.

In an attempt to discover how well this business model works from the clients' perspectives, I decided to use my own system and become a client of my own PR firm. In doing so, I needed to discover what made my firm interesting and sexy to the media. I found that my business's commitment to authentic communication, including maintaining a No-Gossip Zone and achieving work/life balance, was what made us unique.

It wasn't always easy. I did meet with some resistance from the media, my colleagues, clients, and even my employees. Some people just aren't comfortable learning new tricks, and after years of working in a stiff, artificial corporate environment, not everyone could handle becoming part of an authentic communication loop. In fact, even if they knew logically that such communication would make them happier and less stressed, their addiction to gossip and drama drove them to their old destructive patterns and communication hang-ups.

Despite the initial difficulties I encountered, it wasn't long before I had my staff on board and my client roster booming. People love to work and exist in environments where they are appreciated and valued, and that's what authentic communication is all about. It is about giving voice to your emotions and thoughts, then accepting them, moving them, and letting them go.

As basic as these steps are, most of us don't learn them in childhood or our schooling. Instead we learn to hide our emotions and play games of inauthentic communication in which we lie, hide, or discourage the truth about our thoughts and needs. Leaving behind these old broken habits and discovering new and healthy ways to communicate isn't easy, and it is especially complicated in a corporate environment where everyone wants to appear cool, calm, and collected.

However, the results speak for themselves. In just one year of having a No-Gossip Zone and authentic communication policies in place, my clients doubled, as did my employees. The peace and happiness in my personal life and in my office also increased, and I was finally able to become the manager I always wanted to be.

In the process of writing this book, I had a special opportunity to put these philosophies into practice. It truly was a communal effort, as many of my staff contributed their ideas and their words, most notably my coauthor, Bridget Sharkey, and Amanda Aldinger, Empower PR's other writer. It makes sense that we wrote the book together, because we operate as a team in all that we do. However, the voice in this book is that of my own, since I set the tone for Empower PR with these philosophies and practices.

As you read this book, you might find some resistance within yourself. You might find that some part of you strongly rejects the idea of authentic communication and the steps that create it. However, if you recognize this resistance as a persona or a little demon in you that wants to hold on to the "old way of doing things," you can diminish that inner voice's power. You can then transform your life and your career into authentic sources of joy and aliveness, and by doing so, you can emit positive energy that will improve your entire organization. No step is too small and no employee is unimportant—no matter where you stand in the office hierarchy, if you are positive and proactive, the effects will be felt throughout your office.

—Sam Chapman

AN EMPLOYEE'S EXPERIENCE

Most offices that I have worked in seem to thrive on inauthentic communication. From forced small talk to disingenuous friendships to backstabbing, no one behaves as their authentic selves or shares their real emotions. Sadly, people think they have to act this way in order to get ahead in the corporate world. This emotionless robot routine is thought to be as necessary as showing up on time or dressing in business attire, and it is something most of us learn and perfect within our first few months in the "real world."

Of course, this so-called real world is about as fake as it can get. Since you don't know who to trust or how much of yourself you can really share with the people you are surrounded by every day, you often go home feeling stressed, tense, and drained. What an awful way to end the majority of your days!

When I first went in for an interview at Empower PR, I expected to discover a similar type of office environment. Imagine my surprise when one of the first things that Sam asked me was: *When was the last time you cried?* I certainly wasn't expecting such a revealing and emotionally honest question! The rest of the interview continued in the same vein, and I realized that I was in a much different office environment, one where emotional honesty was just as important as hard work.

Authentic communication isn't the only thing that sets our office apart from other offices. Along with (or maybe as a result of) this different environment, we also are all friends. We all spend plenty of time together outside of work as well. We each know everyone's significant others, families, and friends. We celebrate major life events together, from engagements to birthdays to anniversaries to holidays.

Because we all know each other, both inside the office and outside the office, we are better able to communicate and we respect each other as individuals, not just as coworkers. The more we communicate authentically, the more authentic our relationships become and the more authentic our communication becomes! So you can see that once you start the ball of authenticity going, it just mounts and mounts, bringing more creativity and joy into all of your relationships and interactions.

The communication skills I have learned from working at Empower PR aren't relegated to my interactions with my coworkers and clients, nor are they for any employee here. We take home the lessons we learn and use them to our benefit in all of our relationships. Working and living authentically is the only way to work and live happily.

—Bridget Sharkey

The philosophies in this book might take some getting used to at first. However, you will find that each chapter builds upon ideas introduced in earlier chapters, so you can take the book one step at a time. We begin with the No-Gossip Zone, which is quite fitting, as this is where my (Sam's) introduction to authentic communication first began as well.

CHAPTER 1

THE NO-GOSSIP ZONE

What is told in the ear of a man is often heard one hundred miles away.

—Chinese proverb

For most of us, it goes without saying that gossip is a part of any work environment. If people coexist within a work or social situation, they will gossip about one another, right? Because this is such an accepted reality of human communication, it's safe to say that everyone has either been hurt by the gossiping of others, gossiped themselves, or had their words construed in a way that hurt someone else.

In a recent study performed by Randstad Corporation, employees cited office gossip as their number one annoyance in their workplace. Employers also have good reason to curb loose lips, as office gossip takes up to sixty-five hours a year of an employee's time at work, according to a July 2002 survey by Equisys. But it doesn't have to be that way.

Have you ever imagined what your office environment would be like if gossip were banned? If coworkers truly were not able to talk about each other behind their backs and had to call out and sincerely address any individual who was gossiped about in conversation? There would be no more whispering by the communal coffee pot or in the restrooms, no more insidious backstabbing, and certainly no more poisonous secrets. Sounds pretty great, huh?

But how do you effect such a change, especially when gossip seems to surround every part of our personal and professional lives? Indeed, some people believe that gossip is simply part of human nature. However, there is nothing "natural" about communication that is hurtful and has the power to ruin both relationships and reputations. Although it may seem acceptable, the hurtful reality of gossip is something that is a growing issue, especially with the rise of social and interoffice technology. Thankfully, there is a way you and your office can eradicate hurtful gossip, and it is through the No-Gossip Zone.

Office Scene: The Gossipers

The Scene: Zen Marketing, Inc.

The Problem: Gossip

The People: Lucy (a marketing executive), Patty (a marketing associate), Leslie (a marketing associate), Jackie (the CEO), Maggie (the director of marketing)

Zen Marketing, Inc., is a start-up company in Seattle. For the last two years, Jackie has worked nonstop trying to make her company a success, but lately she has been relying more on Lucy and Maggie, her marketing gurus and right-hand associates. In return, Lucy and Maggie have been putting in plenty of hours and working very hard. However, Lucy secretly thinks that she has better ideas than Jackie, and she tries to usurp Jackie's authority every chance she gets.

One of the ways Lucy asserts her secret feelings is by gossiping with Maggie about Jackie's "poor" business decisions. Maggie and Lucy often work late and go to meetings together, so Lucy has plenty of time to gossip and chew Maggie's ear off about her issues with Jackie. Maggie tries to ignore the negative feedback, but it is beginning to overwhelm her.

Meanwhile, when at the office, Lucy spends her free time gossiping to the other employees, including her two friends, Patty and Leslie. Patty and Leslie know that Lucy is a bit of a gossip and a depressed character, but she always manages to lure them into listening to her drawn-out rants about Jackie.

The gossip comes to a head one day when Lucy comes into the office and tells Patty that Jackie is thinking of firing Leslie. Lucy claims that Jackie told her in confidence the night before, and Patty can't resist

4 THE NO-GOSSIP ZONE

the adrenaline rush of knowing such a potent secret. The two gossip about it all morning until they finally decide to tell Leslie at lunch.

When Leslie hears the news, she is dumbfounded and also very angry. She knows that she has been a good employee at Zen, so she doesn't understand why Jackie would do this to her. For the next couple of weeks, Leslie is sullen and bitter, silently waiting for Jackie to give her the ax. After waiting and waiting, she starts to wonder if Lucy spoke out of turn, as Jackie seems to have no intention of firing her.

Tired of the constant gossip circling around the office, Leslie decides to go straight to the source and ask Jackie if the rumors about her being fired are true. Jackie flushes with surprise and anger and says, "Of course not. I told Lucy in confidence that we might need to make cutbacks. But I didn't name names, and I certainly would hate to lose you. You are one of our most promising employees."

Leslie sighs in relief and then admits, "I should have just asked you right away. I can't believe how much time I have spent worrying and being angry."

Jackie agrees, but adds, "I shouldn't have said that to Lucy in the first place. I know what a gossip she is, but more importantly, I should have just been up front with my employees."

Later, Jackie calls Lucy into her office to confront her about the gossip. At first Lucy loudly denies telling Leslie anything, but then she finally admits she spoke out of turn. When Jackie tells her that she needs to stop gossiping or risk losing her job, Lucy flushes and admits she would rather seek a different job with more creative authority. In other words, she isn't ready to stop gossiping.

The rest of Zen Marketing (especially Maggie, Patty, and Leslie) breathes a sigh of relief that Lucy and her toxic gossip are finally leaving the building. Jackie asks everyone to stop gossiping and simply come to her with their concerns from now on. And Lucy? She is still somewhere gossiping; only this time, she's just ruining her own day.

WHAT EXACTLY IS GOSSIP?

Part of the reason that gossip can take over so much of our lives is we don't always realize when we are actively taking part in it. Everyone has different definitions for what gossip is, and even the dictionary seems to offer very dissimilar examples. For instance, Merriam-Webster defines gossip as "chatty talk," while MSN Encarta defines it as "to spread rumors or tell people the personal details of others' lives, especially maliciously."

So which is it? These two drastically different definitions carry very different consequences. The bottom line is this:

> Gossip can be defined as an exchange of negative information between two or more people about someone who isn't present. So unless what you are saying is complimentary, it is best to be avoided. Pretty simple—if it is negative, it is gossip.

HOW GOSSIP HURTS

Gossip is a vice of many people, mainly because it seems to be a victimless crime. Most of the time you never have to see the effects of your gossip, or look the person you were gossiping about in the eye and see how hurt they are. If we did, chances are most of us would never gossip again.

Another reason it is so prevalent is because the definition of gossip is sometimes unclear. Is it gossip when you relay to your coworker that Janie from Accounting is going through a divorce, or is it just "chewing the fat"? Did you have good or bad intentions when discussing Janie's divorce? Were you trying to hurt her reputation, or were you merely whiling away the time with a coworker over a coffee break?

The surprising fact is, the intent rarely makes a difference. Even if you had good intentions when sharing the information, you never know if your listener will have the same good intentions when repeating the information to someone else. Nor do you know how many individuals your listener will decide to tell, despite any purported "promise of secrecy."

Additionally, you have no idea how Janie will feel when she hears that the office has been gabbing about her personal life, and no matter what you said initially, you will have no control over the reports that she hears. Furthermore, even if your intentions are positive, that doesn't mean the information that was originally shared will be communicated correctly.

These points combined present one of the best reasons I can think of for abstaining from gossiping:

> When you gossip, you cannot control the flow of information, either to the general public or to the person you were gossiping about.

Once you have shared information with someone else, the gossip becomes the property of whomever you shared it with, and however they choose to repeat or revise the story is out of your hands. Therefore:

> The only way to be truly safe from such a possible negative outcome is to avoid gossip entirely.

WHY ELIMINATE GOSSIP?

Now consider the excuses you are currently formulating in your head as to why a No-Gossip Zone couldn't possibly be a part of your life. Ask yourself what it is about gossiping that makes you unwilling to remove it from your office and your daily life. Is it because you get a little thrill when you hear private information? Or because you enjoy that moment of superiority when you get to fill someone in on a piece of juicy gossip they haven't heard yet? Perhaps you're someone who feels better when they're on the inside of things, or you like a little something to connect you to everyone around you. Oftentimes, gossip can be a quick and easy way to release negative emotions you're feeling about someone in the office. When something is stewing within you, it certainly feels good to get it off your chest and share it with it someone.

There's nothing wrong with these emotions per se. We all like to feel "in the know" and part of something, but wouldn't it be better to feel like part of a cohesive team and a friendly office? Wouldn't it be better to be "in the know" by not keeping secrets and hiding feelings from your coworkers and, instead, working in an open and authentic environment? When it comes to gossip, for every individual who is "in the know" there's someone who's being completely excluded. And that may include you. In an office where gossip is permitted, no one is exempt from being talked about. Hopefully you're starting to recognize that gossip is really just the means to an unhappy end. Gossip never fulfills what you want it to, and you'd be so much happier with the people you work with if everyone works hard to promote and employ authentic communication all of the time.

CREATING A NO-GOSSIP ZONE

I encountered quite a severe case of gossip in my own office years back. My office, like most PR firms, was full of young, talented professionals who were experts in their fields. Unfortunately, not all of their talent was able to shine, primarily because a few of these employees spent all of their time gossiping about the personal lives of upper management. After getting wind of the situation, I hoped the situation would clear up. But it didn't—instead, it got worse. In fact, it got so bad that I had to fire the ringleader, an otherwise charming and talented young woman who just couldn't resist the appeal of a "juicy bit" of gossip.

Unfortunately, the gossip did not end there. The woman I had fired still had a few friends in the office, and after I discovered that these remaining employees were continuing to gossip (and one even went so far as to divulge confidential client information), I had to fire every individual involved in the situation. It was not an easy choice to make, especially in a tight-knit office environment. But I knew that if I didn't fire those who were instigating the problem, I would never see the end of gossip in my office, nor would I know which of my employees I could actually trust. In order for my company to grow and succeed, I needed to get rid of those whose behavior was holding us back. Therefore, I fired the gossips and never looked back.

However, I knew the process couldn't end there. I realized that my office, like most offices in America, was programmed to accept and encourage gossip. Employers keep secrets from employees; employees keep secrets from one another, and in the end the entire office becomes riddled with "did you hear" and "listen to this" types of conversations, with very few individuals ever fully knowing the initial source or truth of the matter. The only way to stop this trend is to turn the workplace into a complete and total No-Gossip Zone.

A NO-GOSSIP ZONE POLICY
- A formal agreement among all employees (either verbal or written) to not participate in gossip
- An agreement to identify and stop gossip when it is heard
- An agreement to "follow up" with the person who was being gossiped about and share what was said
- An ongoing commitment to reveal one's true feelings, thoughts, and desires within the work environment, thereby removing any need or environment for gossip

As an employer, introducing the No-Gossip Zone requires some tact. Some people believe that free speech means they can say whatever they want, regardless of who it hurts or whether or not it is truthful. Thus, instead of introducing the no-gossip policy as a requirement, give employees the option to gossip and leave, or not gossip and stay. As a manager, you have the right and even the responsibility to monitor the environment that your employees work in, so put the choice to your office simply: toe the no-gossip line, or be prepared for the consequences.

Within my own office I made the choice to simply ask for a verbal agreement from my employees not to gossip. However, employers can opt for a signed agreement stating that employees pledge not to gossip. This means if they do gossip, they will be prepared for the consequences. This can be a helpful precaution from a legal standpoint, such as if an employee under contract gets fired for gossip but tries to claim ignorance of the policy.

Depending on the size of your office, it might make sense to have one large group meeting or to have several small meetings separated by job responsibilities. (In other words, you could break employees into groups based on departments. This makes sense, because chances are these are the people who work closely together and with whom they potentially would encounter gossip.) Employees do not just have the responsibility to avoid gossip at all costs. They also have the responsibility to call out gossip whenever they hear it. First, they must confront the gossiper and address the gossip in some form or another. Second, they must go to the person who was being gossiped about to reveal what they heard. The gossiper also has the responsibility to confess their gossip to the person they were talking about. With this system the gossip victim's awareness that the gossiper will be following up with them will encourage the gossiper to be honest. Believe it or not, the gossip victim will no doubt be pleased with the honesty they are being shown. Although they might be a little miffed at what they hear, they will also be relieved to know that the gossip was cut short and reported back to them in its entirety.

Some observant readers might wonder: *Isn't going to the person who was being gossiped about and reporting the gossip...well, gossip?* Not at all! Because in a No-Gossip Zone, the gossiper is well aware that their gossip is being reported, and the person reporting the gossip will feel compelled to stick to the facts. Furthermore, the individual who is reporting the gossip is not secretly relaying information to one person behind the back of another. They are reporting factual information directly to *one* individual with the singular intention of halting gossipy behavior.

> Openness and truth stop gossip in its devious tracks.

THE BENEFITS OF A NO-GOSSIP ZONE

In an ideal work environment, the practice of hearing and reporting gossip needn't occur very often. An ideal no-gossip office environment entirely removes the original need for gossip.

> By creating an environment where employees and employers can share their open, honest, and authentic feelings with one another, the need for gossip will be eradicated.

Although authentic communication in the workplace is not easy, it is possible and the results are undeniably positive. Instituting authentic communication as the means of interoffice communication will take some work and does present its challenges. But when people feel safe sharing their feelings and are content in knowing their needs are being cared for, the malice and sadness that create gossip will cease to exist.

ENCOUNTERING RESISTANCE

When I first implemented a no-gossip policy in my office, I encountered plenty of feedback from my colleagues. Some scoffed at the idea that I could effectively remove gossip from the office. How can you possibly control what people are saying when no one is looking? Others thought I had no right to limit the freedom of speech of my employees. Still others said gossip was human nature and had to be accepted as a natural part of life.

On the road to implementing a no-gossip policy you will likely encounter some or all of the excuses below. Here are strategies for addressing each:

"It can't be done!"

Yes, it can. You just need to be firm. If an employee won't stop gossiping, then, as a last resort, their employment is terminated. To that end, I am proud to say that since this policy was officially instituted, I haven't had to fire a single employee. Employees are aware of this policy when they start at Empower PR, and they agree to it as part of our better business practices. If they regularly renege on this promise, they are given a verbal warning. If they renege again, they are gone!

> No gossip becomes more than just a choice; it becomes a job requirement.

And if it's a job requirement, no one wants to be the one person who feels he or she is above the requirements of the job. Also, it would be a terrible tragedy for an employee to lose a job over something as petty and shallow as gossiping about coworkers. Who wants to be known as the office gossip?

"But what about freedom of speech?"

If workplace speech were entirely free and without any consequences whatsoever, you could tell your boss to go jump in a lake, or tell a client that their service was worthless. But of course you don't do these things, because you know there would be negative repercussions in the end. The same is true for office gossip. Gossip is rife with negative repercussions, and no smart business owner who wants the highest quality of work from his employees as well as positive interpersonal relations within the office would allow his or her company to run on a model of negativity and deceit. Freedom of speech gives you the right to express your mind, and if that type of expression goes outside the bounds of what's acceptable in the office, then you must be prepared to freely accept the consequences.

"It's human nature!"

You could argue that a lot of things are human nature—laziness, lethargy, jealousy, pettiness—but are those qualities allowed to run rampant in the office? No way. Just because something is common and frequent doesn't mean it is forever ingrained in our nature. We have the power to choose and define our character, both inside and outside the workplace. Excusing poor behavior as human nature underestimates society as a whole. Especially in a situation where success is the key goal, such as in a work environment, it's important that policies exist prohibiting behaviors that prevent the company from achieving its goals.

- Gossip has the power to bring down the mood of the entire office, as well as ruin reputations and decrease productivity.
- It is possible to remove gossip from the office, as long as everyone agrees to follow a no-gossip policy.
- If people can't stop gossiping, they have to face the consequences. Being part of a healthy and authentic work environment is part of being a good employee.

CHAPTER 2

BE REAL

AUTHENTIC COMMUNICATION
AS A KEY SUCCESS FACTOR

What a wee little part of a person's life are his acts and his words! His real life is led in his head, and is known to none but himself.

—Mark Twain

Removing gossip from the workplace is just one step in creating a work environment of authentic communication. Authentic communication allows for feedback and improvement of the team and of the company and will create an environment where everyone's needs and desires can be met. An overall spirit of honesty and informed communication patterns allow us to best serve our clients.

The same policy of authentic communication is needed when it comes to employee relations. Withholding feedback and not coming clean about what is true for you allows for negativity to fester and worsen by the day. As long as we can clearly understand the difference between authentic communication and criticism (and understand that certain types of communication, such as that of a sexual nature, are not appropriate in the workplace), then creating an environment of open, authentic communication is the key to a successful, enjoyable work environment.

Office Scene: When Withholds Take Over the Office

The Scene: Barnaby Collections, LLC

The Problem: Inauthentic communication

The People: Carrie (the office manger), Gerry (the CEO), Jim (Carrie's assistant)

Barnaby Collections is a small firm that specializes in retrieving funds for companies worldwide. Gerry started the firm a few years ago after leaving a toxic office environment at another firm, and since then he has focused on hiring only positive, upbeat people. He believes in hard work, but he also wants his employees to have fun and be happy. Most importantly, he wants his employees to like him, so he goes out of his way to make sure he is the office favorite.

Unfortunately, Gerry's merry attitude doesn't always work very well for management purposes. Whenever there is a problem in the office, whether it is a tight deadline or a coworker disagreement, Gerry often tries to avoid taking a managerial stance. He doesn't want to have to be the bad guy and crack down on anybody, so he usually just lets his employees do as they please. As a result, employees who are hardworking and committed to making their clients happy end up doing the majority of the work in order to pick up the slack for less motivated employees.

Carrie is one such hardworking employee. She has known Gerry for years (they worked together at Gerry's previous firm), and she has always enjoyed his company. She thought she would love working for such a fun-loving, friendly guy. However, after just a few months at Barnaby Collections, she discovers the opposite is true. Since Gerry is always trying to be everyone's friend, he never behaves as a boss, and he certainly never asks people to stay late or cut back on their lunchtime, with the result that she works late hours to finish projects by herself.

Jim is an example of one of the employees who takes advantage of Gerry's lax managerial attitude. Whenever Gerry asks him to do something, Jim barely takes notice. He spends most of his time on the computer, surfing the Web, and he also calls in sick often. Carrie is left to do his dirty work, including tasks that she doesn't have the time to do, meaning she goes home late, tired, and cranky. Rather than tell Gerry how she feels about Jim's performance and his own performance as a boss, Carrie has decided to look for another job.

When Gerry gets wind of Carrie's job search via the rumor mill, he is very hurt and angry. He calls Carrie into his office to find out what is going on.

"Carrie, I assume you know why I asked you in here today," he says.

"Well, I guess so. Rob told me you found out I was looking for another job," says Carrie coolly.

Her detached demeanor stuns Gerry. "Yes, but I don't understand. We have been friends for years. If you were unhappy here, why didn't you tell me?"

Carrie scoffs and then suddenly finds all the pent-up frustration pouring out of her. She yells, "What on earth are you talking about? Why would I need to tell you that I am not happy working sixty hours a week while your 'buddy' Jim works half of that? I am tired of picking up the slack here and not getting to put my kids to bed, all because you don't want to be the bad guy and lay down the law!"

Gerry sits there, silent and stunned. "I had no idea you were working that much," he begins, but Carrie interrupts.

"And you call me your friend!" she says. "If you were my friend, you should have noticed how miserable and tired I was. You should have known that I couldn't even find time to see my mother in the hospital last month, all because Jim decided to call in sick four days in a row!"

Gerry, who is now getting upset, snaps back, "No, I shouldn't notice those things! You should have spoken up and told me what was happening with you. I didn't even know your mother was in the hospital. Nor did I know that Jim called in sick four days in a row. These are things you should tell me. You say I am not a good manager, but it sounds like you haven't done much better with Jim. If only you would have told me, maybe things could have been different."

"It's too late now," says Carrie.

"It's never too late to hear what's going on with my friends, least of all you," says Gerry. "Tell me more about what's happening here, and I vow to fix it, any way I can. Together we can make sure that you get to spend time with your family, and that Jim starts pulling his weight."

Carrie smiles. "That's why I love you, Gerry. You really are a great friend. I should have known I could come to you instead of hiding how I really felt!"

COMMUNICATING AUTHENTICALLY WITH CLIENTS

Perhaps the trickiest part of authentic communication in the workplace is perfecting the art of authentic speech with clients. American business tradition tells us that the "customer is always right," and most service providers go to any lengths to flatter and sweet-talk their clients. Often we do this at the expense of authentic communication, and we are forced to squelch what is true for us. However, denying honest feedback in the name of client satisfaction is actually counterproductive.

> Indeed, in our efforts to please the client at all costs, we often end up doing them a disservice.

Why?

Because the creation and maintenance of authentic relationships among peers is the most valuable role a service provider can bestow upon a client. Yes-men, patsies, and sycophants do not give great service to their clients or to their own bottom line, because they don't know how to constructively advise their clients in ways that will make them more successful.

> Your client has come to you because you have a skill set that they do not possess, and they need your help to expand their business and create higher levels of success for their company.

If all you do is give them ill advice because you're too afraid to tell them when something may not be working the right way, then you aren't fully doing your job, and your clients won't reach their full potential.

No one gets ahead in life by creating false relationships and weak business decisions—and any business decision is weak if it is not driven by truth.

Inauthentic communication or "pretending" doesn't work well, especially in my field, public relations. For example, if a client doesn't perform well on television, she needs to know because her poor performance affects both her business and your business. Pretending as if she successfully executed her television pitch hurts both your client and your firm. The public won't be interested in investing in your client's product, and your company will look as if it's given poor representation. Therefore, to communicate inauthentically with your client—and, by proxy, the public—defeats the purpose of your contract.

At Empower PR we make it a policy to always be honest with our clients, no matter how tough it might be at times. For example, if our client has an idea that we know from our public relations experience to be poor, we tell them so in a straightforward manner. We don't just go ahead and use the bad idea anyway, assuming that the customer is king, because when the idea goes nowhere and the publicity campaign fails, our client is going to want to know why. Before the money and time are wasted, we stop a bad idea in its tracks (no matter who came up with it) and get the good ideas rolling. Of course it isn't easy to look a client in the face and tell them "I don't think so," but it's better than risking your own reputation with your client and with the media.

After all, clients do not hire a business because they are interested in how well its people can salute. Anyone can be obedient—it doesn't take any special talent or creativity to toe the line. A service provider must provide more than humble obedience; it's necessary that it provide the service the client is paying for. Helping your client grow and change creates a valuable and lasting relationship that will foster both monetary and emotional returns.

A good way to begin an authentic relationship with your client is to announce your intentions to do so at the start of your contract. I use the fact that I communicate authentically with everyone as part of my initial sales pitch, and, believe it or not, my commitment to honesty has actually earned me a number of clients. If you are already in the midst of your relationship, you can initiate authentic communication simply by announcing your intention to be honest and up-front and then share your feedback.

You can follow this with your employees as well. I use the interview process as an opportunity to explain to potential new hires our policy of no gossip and authentic communication, and I see if it is an environment they would support. If not, our office is not a good fit for them.

COMMUNICATING AUTHENTICALLY WITH EMPLOYEES

As a manager, I have found that blocking what you are feeling or thinking makes everyone and everything in the office tense and uncomfortable. Sharing my disappointments allows my employees to shift and allows me to adjust my feelings and move on.

Authentic communication isn't just necessary for those lower on the totem pole. It must be welcomed all along the chain of command.

> Managers have to be open to extending authentic communication to their employees, and they also have to be open to hearing authentic communication from their employees.

Needless to say, all of the communication won't be positive. If all feedback were positive all of the time, then there would never be any reason to strive for better or to change tactics in order to create new results. So the issue is not whether you have negative feedback or are displeased with a coworker, it's learning how to authentically communicate in a way that speaks truthfully but doesn't intentionally hurt feelings or shut someone down. By opening themselves up to the truth, managers can create a 360-degree loop of communication within the office, with a give-and-take of feedback that benefits everyone, from the temp in the mailroom to the president of the company.

THE ADVANCED PROGRAM OF AUTHENTIC COMMUNICATION

Once you and your colleagues perfect the small steps of authentic communication with one another individually, you will be ready for an advanced placement course involving the office community as a whole. The advanced placement version of authentic communication involves everyone in your office sitting down together and working as a group to implement authentic communication techniques as a way of communicating as a company. You will learn many authentic communication tools throughout this book, all of which will help you to become an expert in this arena.

This process begins by individually sharing what you have withheld from one another. Once everyone has taken their turn releasing their withholds (both big and small), then the hidden feelings will be out in the open, allowing everyone in the office to be on the same page. It's important that once you begin the office-wide advanced program you continue it with weekly meetings that focus solely on your employees' mental processes and individual feelings. These meetings must remain separate from other work meetings, where the focus is on work and weekly progress reports.

Implementing this program sends a strong message to your employees, communicating to them that you value them as individuals with emotions and feelings rather than automatons who exist simply to crank out work and build accounts. Giving them a forum where they're allowed and encouraged to authentically communicate in a safe environment shows that you care about their mental health and how they're feeling as a member of your company. Showing them how much you value their work will also do wonders to increase company morale and, in effect, their work ethic. Who doesn't enjoy feeling like they are a part of something where their contributions and input matter? I'm not sure I know anyone who doesn't begin to get discouraged when they feel as if they exist solely to work within confines that don't include their emotional or personal well-being.

To ensure the success of this program, it's advised that you look into finding a facilitator to host the meeting. After all, the very reason these problems exist is because humans, in general, have issues communicating authentically, especially in a work environment. Including someone who is a professional will help to make this process effective and successful, and it will duly prove to your employees how seriously you feel about making sure they're able to authentically communicate within the workplace. It also ensures that the meeting has a sense of neutrality, by bringing someone in who doesn't have biased feelings about what goes on in the office.

For assistance finding the right facilitator for your meeting, see "Life Coaches," page 179, for a list of life coaches and therapists.

- People can't read your mind, especially people who don't know you very intimately, such as coworkers and clients. Indeed, even those people who know you the best, such as your family and close friends, still can't know everything you are thinking and feeling.
- If you want to improve your relationships and hence your life, you need to speak up and give voice to your hidden stories and emotions. Only then can you have authentic and healthy relationships.

CHAPTER 3

CHECKING YOUR PERSONAS

I AM MYSELF

Be yourself; everyone else is already taken.

—Oscar Wilde

Who are you today?

It might seem like a silly question. But the truth is, most of us spend our entire lives trapped in one "persona" or another. Rather than act as our authentic selves, we play a false role in an attempt to better serve our emotional needs, both inside and outside the office.

Those roles can vary greatly. Perhaps when you arrive at the office every day, you put on the face that you think your boss and coworkers *want* to see rather than that of who you truly are when you're at home or with your friends. This isn't entirely negative and will normally happen to some extent due to the fact that the work environment has different requirements than the home environment. But in order to communicate authentically and effectively at work, it's important to check your persona and to evaluate how those around you truly see you.

Office Scene: Personas on Parade

The Scene: Hopleaf and Mannon Advertising Agency

The Problem: Communicating through personas rather than one's authentic self

The People: Nelly (an executive), Angela (a new associate), Greg (a coworker), Thomas (the CEO)

Nelly has worked at the Hopleaf and Mannon Advertising Agency for the past fourteen years. During her tenure, she has worked incredibly hard and her many accomplishments and successes have effectively impressed the higher-ups. As a result of her professional success, Nelly has been promoted to an executive with a corner office. For the most part, Nelly loves her job and she considers her coworkers to be true friends. Her interpersonal communication with employees at work had been fine, until recently.

A few months ago, a young associate named Angela started working in Nelly's department. Nelly never gave Angela much thought before, but lately Nelly *has* been noticing Angela, because within the past year she has received not one, but *two* promotions—promotions that Nelly is quite sure Angela does not deserve.

Upset and dismayed over what she views to be favoritism, Nelly spends many a night drowning her sorrows at the local pub with her coworker and close friend, Greg. While Nelly laments her situation, Greg spends the majority of their time together bolstering Nelly's ego and assuring her that she is still Hopleaf and Mannon's number one employee.

Despite Greg's best efforts, Nelly feels blindsided by Angela over and over again. Sometimes it comes in the form of perceived favoritism, like one of the bosses inviting Angela to lunch. Other times Nelly judges what Angela wears and is offended by her character and what she views to be a lack of professionalism. No matter what, it eventually escalates to a point that everything Angela does drives Nelly absolutely mad.

Even though Nelly is undoubtedly at the top of her game as far as her work goes, she dreads coming into the office every day. She loathes the sight of Angela chatting it up with any of the clients, and she despises listening to Angela's so-called brilliant ideas during weekly brainstorming meetings. But while Nelly spends her time making scathing judgments, Angela wonders why the formerly friendly Nelly has become increasingly distant, and why Greg seems to be avoiding her as well.

Finally, after one particularly tense meeting, the company's CEO, Thomas, intervenes. He pulls Nelly aside and asks her why she has been acting so bizarrely as of late. Ashamed that her negative behavior is permeating the office, Nelly hems and haws until she finally admits, "I'm sorry, Thomas, but I've been having a real problem with Angela. I know you all think that she is so great and such a fabulous asset to the company, but I don't understand why she has everything handed to her. I've worked very, very hard to get where I am today. I've stayed late. I've spent my weekends perfecting projects and compiling reports. I've made the decision, time and time again, to forgo a social life in lieu of my work and the success of the company. And now, ten years later, along comes Angela, who has never worked late a day in her life, being promoted! I don't understand it, and I just think it's wrong."

Concerned with Nelly's outburst, and the fact that she'd obviously been withholding these emotions for quite a while, Thomas replies, "I had no idea you felt so strongly, Nelly. I thought you liked Angela's work. You never complained about it before."

"I know," says Nelly. "And I tried to see what everyone else is obviously seeing, but that doesn't mean I think she should be promoted for no reason."

"Well, it's not for no reason, Nelly. Angela is a very hard worker and very talented. She is a great asset to this company. You know that. What's really bothering you?"

"Well," she says, as she is finally forced to examine the truth of her outburst, "I guess I just feel like I'm going to be passed over. This young girl is zipping up the ranks before my very eyes. Before I know it, I will be out the door."

"Are you crazy? You helped build this company, Nelly. No one can ever take that away from you. And no one wants to. But that doesn't mean you get to be the only smart woman around here. We want all of our employees to be intelligent and successful. Why are you so committed to being the only successful woman here?" Thomas asks.

In that moment, Nelly realizes his words are true. She is so caught up in the persona of a smart, successful woman that it makes her angry to have competition on that front. And despite how much she initially wanted Angela to fail, it is true that she is smart and capable. Nelly is shocked to learn that she almost let her own "successful, independent woman" persona stand in the way of Angela's career path.

As she tells Greg about her breakthrough, he realizes that he too has been letting his "helpful friend" persona get in the way of actually *helping* Nelly. Rather than fessing up and telling Nelly the truth (that he actually kind of likes Angela, and that Nelly needs to worry about her own life and leave Angela alone), he routinely sat and listened to Nelly whine and moan. He let her play the victim so he could play the hero, but in the end the only person who could save Nelly was herself.

In an effort to show goodwill, Nelly invites Angela out to lunch the next day, and she discovers that Angela is just as bright and smart as everyone said she is. And, rather than feel threatened, Nelly decides to help foster her ideas and creativity, just the way that a coworker of hers had helped to mentor her decades before.

Once Nelly is able to let go of her persona, she is able to foster a real connection with Angela and let go of the bitterness and envy that was getting in the way of her work. Nelly's working environment improves tenfold, *and* she gains a newfound respect for her coworker as well as a new friend.

WHAT ARE PERSONAS?

In order to better understand the concept of personas, let's examine the three most common personas that we have all experienced in our lives: these are "victim," "villain," and "hero," otherwise known as the Karpman Drama Triangle.

THE DRAMA TRIANGLE:

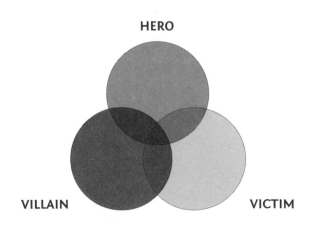

HERO

VILLAIN   VICTIM

Throughout interactions we often assume one of these three personas, sometimes even alternating between them mid-conversation.

VICTIM

You know you are in a victim role when you approach an argument from a "poor me" stance. Victims purport helplessness, often beginning sentences with phrases such as "I can't" or "I don't know." Victims decline responsibility for their own life situation and see things as "happening" to them and them alone, as opposed to being the result of something they've caused. They believe someone or something is responsible for their sadness, anger, etc. They often feel powerless to change anything and experience great anger, fear, and sadness over it. During a fight, the victim may also cower or close down so as to avoid conflict. In general, the victim feels victimized by the world and tends to not take responsibility for their own actions or emotions.

VILLAIN

When you are in a villain persona, you attack, accuse, or otherwise behave aggressively in an argument. You are confrontational and quick to point the finger. A villain takes an argument from 0 to 60 in 2.5 seconds. There is no such thing as a minor argument with a villain—until you admit that they are right, they will continue escalating the fight to the next level. The villain is manipulative, argumentative, and very difficult to have an actual shared conversation with.

HERO

This is a very popular role among busy professionals. Do you know any coworkers or employees who "do it all" and revel in the fact that they are overscheduled to the max? They just love to have "so much work to do" that they're always on their BlackBerrys. Or there's just no time for anything because there's always another meeting, another big project, another hefty component of living the busy, successful, working person's life. A hero behaves as a martyr, piling on responsibilities and refusing help in order to feel superior or needed. A hero can also behave as a martyr by piling on emotional responsibilities, such as always catering to the needs of her coworkers and ignoring her own needs. Heroes will often put everyone else's needs before their own and will do anything, just so they can think of themselves as unselfish. During an argument, the hero will often defer to the other person in order to keep the peace, or they will resist being honest so as to not risk hurting their partner's feelings.

These three personas are closely linked to one another, and indeed each persona requires one of the other two to survive. It's not possible for someone to fully inhabit their persona without feeding off of one of the others. (For example, a victim persona can't survive without a villain persona to persecute them or a hero persona to rescue them.) People inhabiting these personas can alternate between these roles mid-conversation, or they can take on more than one persona at a time—such as a victim who is a passive-aggressive villain, or a hero who is secretly an attention-seeking victim.

If these roles still don't sound familiar to you, read this example of a typical workplace conversation in which the Drama Triangle runs amok:

Kate: I can't believe I have to work late again tonight! This always happens to me.

Jeff: That's rough! You've been here late every night this week.

Kate: Yeah, it's all thanks to Brendan. He completely forgot about our presentation today and now I have to cover for him—as usual.

Jeff: Don't worry. I am sure you will be able to make up for it. Your presentations are always great.

Kate: Well, I wish someone else would notice that. I haven't gotten a raise in six months, but I work harder than almost everyone here.

Jeff: Tell me about it. Sometimes I feel management around here gives a lot of credit to those who really don't deserve it. Like, Janet—she's late every single day!

Kate: Don't even get me started on her. I feel like I'm constantly picking up her slack, too!

Jeff: Yesterday I had to help her figure out how to use Excel. But that's what I do here it seems—train the incompetent people who get hired.

Do you notice how Kate and Jeff switch roles throughout the conversation in order to get their emotional needs met? Or how they respond to each other's emotional needs by switching roles? For instance, when Kate goes into victim role, Jeff becomes a hero. By the end of the conversation, both Kate and Jeff have changed roles numerous times.

But the most amazing thing is, in the end neither of them leaves the conversation feeling any better! The reason is:

> Conversations in persona can often be very draining and emotionally exhausting, because more often than not you're not admitting how you actually feel.

Constantly changing roles and tactics in order to get yourself noticed or appreciated drains both you and your listener of aliveness. When you are alive in your communication, you are authentic and in the moment. Aliveness is responding honestly and engaging the other individual in your thoughts and responses, rather than just auto-responding via the constraints of your persona. Despite the lack of authenticity and satisfaction from such conversations, most people don't know of better ways to communicate. Thus their lives in the office (and at home) become a merry-go-round of personas and dead-end arguments.

We think that we need to squash or hide the worst parts of ourselves, or that we need to be entirely pleasing to everyone we interact with. We don't want to show the world our jealousy, self-righteousness, or bitterness, because we know these are not admirable qualities to have, and they are certainly not admirable qualities to exhibit in the workplace. Yet when we repress natural emotions of sadness, anger, and fear, they simply fester inside of us and we may become stuck.

The fact of the matter is, we all emote and we all react to situations individually. The fact that we feel and emote is inarguable and cannot be controlled. It is when these emotions are always funneled through a persona rather than dealt with authentically that problems begin to occur. Without an outlet for expression, these emotions soon become blockages inside of us, detracting from our health, creativity, and peace of mind.

The best way to get out of your persona and back to authentic communication is to recognize that you are in a persona. Only when you become conscious of the fact that you are in a persona can you move out of it.

IDENTIFY YOUR PERSONAS

The first step is to recognize what personas you put on. We all have our own "stories" that we tell ourselves and each other about who we are and what our position is in the office. We might not use the terms "victim," "villain," or "hero," but we do use euphemisms to describe our personalities in the office. An employee who identifies herself as a hard worker who never leaves the office before nightfall is playing the hero persona, while an employee who never takes responsibility and always has a sob story to excuse their poor performance is a victim.

Though it is very easy to recognize personas in others, it can be a little tricky to recognize personas in ourselves, usually because we don't like to look too closely at our own issues. And even when we do recognize what lies behind our different personas, that doesn't mean it's easy to change the way we communicate.

What's the solution? Bring these personas to the surface! The next time you feel yourself slipping into a persona, don't try to conceal it. Instead, embrace it and play with it! Persona play is a great way to get familiar with your personas and even have fun with these otherwise unpleasant drifts. Understand your personas on a more individual basis. Give yourself and your personality some dimension by recognizing the different personas and give them names and easily recognizable attributes. Here are a few examples of common personas:

Mr. Right: This persona is often taken on when someone wants to feel in control in an otherwise uncertain world. Mr. Right refuses to accept other people's points of view or hear others' ideas. This persona is always correct and cannot be reasoned with or convinced otherwise.

Pleaser: Pleaser hates to say the word "no." She hates to turn down assignments, ask for help, or express doubt or resistance. She tries to do everything in her power to please and impress her boss, even if it means that her own peace of mind or relationships outside the office suffer. A people pleaser to the extreme, if someone wants it done she'll do it. No matter what the cost.

Lazy Larry: As the name suggests, Lazy Larry hates to do more than the bare minimum on the job. He doesn't think his job should ever interfere with his social life, and is insulted whenever he doesn't get to leave the office on time. Lazy, unmotivated, and not interested in furthering his career or fulfilling his job responsibilities, he's pretty much here to do the time, collect the paycheck, and go home.

Me Me: Me Me can't get enough attention, as her name implies. She has to insert her two cents into every conversation she comes across, even if she has no idea what she is talking about. Her self-importance derives from having an opinion on everything and making sure she is being acknowledged. As long as she is center stage, she is happy—even if it means walking all over other people in order to get the spotlight.

Martyr Mary: This persona acts put upon and taken advantage of by everyone in her life, from the people in her office to the lady at Starbucks to the people on her bus route. Martyr Mary can't catch a break—and she wants you to know about it! There's truly no convincing her that she can take control of her own fate, and she's perfectly content to drown herself (and everyone around her) in her sorrows. Feeding into her stories and legitimizing her claims only fuels the fire. Don't let her dreary demeanor fool you; she loves nothing more than her sob stories!

Do any of these personas sound like you, or someone you work with? When you recognize your personas, don't hide them or try to change them. Instead, bring them to the surface and work to turn them into something more authentic. By acting out your personas to the max, you can keep from becoming overly attached to them, as you will recognize them for what they are—mere roles. And since you are in a role, why not act it out to the fullest?

When you find yourself in a persona, you can act it out to the extreme. Adopt a certain way of speaking (e.g., Mr. Right speaks very forcefully, Pleaser speaks in sugar-sweet tones), and maybe even certain mannerisms (Lazy Larry yawns a lot, Me Me has grandiose movements). Make it into a performance (after all, that is basically what it is!). Let your office mates know what you're up to, and encourage them to play with their personas as well.

Although your personas can be harmful if they remain unchecked, it's important that you don't deride them or feel guilty when you are in a persona. There is nothing inherently wrong with your personas. Most of them actually come from places of love and positive energy. For example, a Mr. Right persona actually comes from a person wanting things to be orderly and peaceful, and a Me Me persona comes from a person's need to be loved and noticed. Nothing is wrong with these needs. It is just when these needs get out of hand and become masked under inauthentic emotions and communication patterns that these personas become problematic.

When you love your personas, flaws and all, you can shift out of them easily. You can see them from an objective standpoint without anger and sadness. This means you can disconnect from them while still maintaining a positive outlook.

Once you recognize your personas and embrace them, you can then move on to the next step—controlling them!

DRIFT AND SHIFT: GETTING OUT OF A PERSONA

Is it ever possible to communicate authentically 100% of the time? Sadly, no. As imperfect creatures, we are always going to drift away from authentic communication and slip into old patterns and habits. For some of us, this might mean we drift into a persona like Mr. Right; for others it might mean we drift into an emotion like sadness and get stuck there all day long.

But don't worry—this drifting is natural and part of the process of authentic communication. In fact, you will be drifting all day long, but you hopefully will be shifting as well.

When you shift you recognize that you are caught in a persona or stuck in an emotion. Just by realizing that you have drifted, you can begin to shift back to authentic communication. When you see that you are playing a role rather than being authentic, you can shift from a "victim" persona back into your authentic essence, or the ease and flow of life. When you discover that you are being Mr. Right, you can relax your grasp and begin shifting back to reality.

It doesn't matter how many times a day you drift (although you will most likely drift less and less the more you practice authentic communication).

> All that matters is that you continually notice your drifts and make an effort to shift, which you can do by recognizing your drift and acting on it.

Let's look at some ways you can put the shift into action.

PHYSICAL SHIFTING

Often when we are drifting emotionally, our bodies reflect it. You might sweat, cross your arms, shake your leg, or bite your nails. Whatever the case, when your inner self is in distress, your outer self will show evidence of this.

The great news is the opposite is also true. When you shift yourself physically, you can also help shift yourself emotionally. So the next time you are stuck in a bad mood, try changing your body language. Uncross your arms, wipe the frown off your face, and try shaking the stress out of your body physically. You might look a little crazy to passersby, but no doubt your mind will shift as a result of this physical change.

To help you remember to shift out of your drifts, try tacking up this phrase near your workspace or computer:

SHIFT YOUR DRIFT!

- We all have personas that we slip into during communication. These personas serve a hidden need inside of us (a need to be appreciated, a need to be validated, etc.). However, if you are authentic about these needs, you are more likely to get them met and much more likely to have a happy work environment.
- The most common personas are victim, villain, and hero, and they all contribute to workplace miscommunication and can lead to gossip.
- In order to begin to get out of a persona, simply notice and admit that you are in a persona and not communicating authentically.

CHAPTER 4

GETTING "UNSTUCK"

MASTERING YOUR EMOTIONS IN THE OFFICE

Emotion is the chief source of consciousness. There is no change from darkness to light or from inertia to movement without emotion.

—Carl Gustav Jung

According to Drs. Gay and Kathlyn Hendricks, there are five authentic emotions. They are *fear, sadness, anger, joy,* and *sexual attraction.* All emotions inside the workplace (and outside the workplace, for that matter) are combinations of these five emotions. For instance, frustration over the copier being on the fritz is probably a mixture of anger and perhaps fear (such as, "What's going to happen if I don't get this report printed in time?"). Job dissatisfaction stems from feelings of sadness ("Why doesn't my boss appreciate me?") and anger ("Why do I have to waste my life at a job I hate?").

By deciphering which of the five key emotions are contributing to your current state of mind, you will be better able to understand your own situation. Instead of thinking, "I am having a bad day because this place is a nightmare!" you will think, "I am feeling sad because my ideas were passed over in a meeting." This alert self-awareness helps you cue into your real emotions and discover what (if anything) you can do to improve your situation.

If you are able to correctly identify what exactly is making you feel as if your office is a nightmare rather than sitting with those feelings all day long, you'll be able to reframe your point of view. If you know it's because you are sad that your ideas were passed over, then you can write your ideas down and pledge to assert yourself better at the next meeting, take extra pains to share your ideas with management and your coworkers, or just let it go and come up with something new and fresh for next time.

If you are having trouble identifying your emotion, sit down and close your eyes. Breathing deeply in and out, try to determine where the emotion is located in your body. Anger usually causes tension in the back, whereas fear tends to reside in the stomach, and sadness is often felt in the throat or behind the eyes. Locate where the emotion is residing in you, and ask yourself what is really happening inside of you. Look for the root cause that is leading to the emotion—you might be surprised by what you find.

Office Scene: Moving It Forward

The Scene: Anders Consulting, Inc.

The Problem: Not moving your emotions

The People: Jan (a consultant), Dan (the CEO), Tara (a coworker)

Jan has been working at Anders Consulting, Inc., for just under a year. During that time she has been in charge of numerous accounts and has been quite successful in her consulting responsibilities. But throughout it all, Jan simply hasn't been able to shake the label of herself as the "new girl." The other consulting associates and executives have multiple years of experience working with Anders Consulting, and even though everyone is welcoming to Jan, she hates feeling like one of the new kids.

Because of her insecurities, Jan often goes out of her way to impose her importance on others and offer her own two cents. Regardless of how little she knows about the topic, Jan often steals the focus at company meetings, making sure everyone hears about her years of experience and her take on whatever situation is currently at hand. Needless to say, she is fast becoming everyone's least favorite coworker. As more people pull away from her and avoid her, Jan's imposing behavior intensifies the more she struggles to belong and to be liked.

After a few months of this roundabout cycle, Jan becomes convinced that everyone in the office hates her. Sometimes people won't even make eye contact with her when she is speaking. At this point, most of the employees feel like Jan is a bad fit for the office. Her bragging and loudmouthed behavior has driven her to become what she feared the most—the office outcast.

Seeing the damage that is resulting from his employees' stuck behavior, the CEO of Anders Consulting, Dan, calls in a mediator to help the opposing factions come to a truce.

At the meeting the mediator tells the office that rather than continuing to assume possible motives and apply negative stories to every behavior, the coworkers and Jan need to sit down and actually talk out their problems with one another. Taking the mediator's advice, they sit down in a circle and are encouraged to vent all of their issues. Though nervous at first, one of Jan's coworkers raises her hand and speaks directly to Jan: "I hate it when you take credit for things you didn't do. I hate when you speak over me in the meeting. And most of all, I hate it that you always have to make yourself the center of attention." Jan, red-faced and teary-eyed, at first rejects these feelings, saying, "I never do that! I don't do that! I admit I am a talker, but since when is that a crime?"

A different coworker, Tara, chimes in. "No one has a problem with you being talkative. In fact, when you first started here, it was one of the things I enjoyed most about you. But now all you do is talk! You never listen or have a conversation—you just get in the spotlight and stay there. Why is that?"

Jan flushes. "It was really hard for me to come in here and be the only new person. I really, really wanted to fit in. But you guys seemed so tight-knit. Half of the time I didn't even know what you guys were talking about. Everything seemed to revolve around inside jokes and references to people I've never met. So I tried to become part of the group by adding my own conversation and my own two cents to whatever you all were discussing. I guess it backfired."

Tara looks guilty and admits, "It's true we didn't welcome you in the best way. But I had no idea that the reason you behaved like that was because you wanted to fit in. I thought you were acting like that because you thought you were better than us."

Jan starts crying slowly. "No way! How could you think that? I just wanted to fit in and belong. Isn't that what we all want?"

For the rest of the afternoon, Jan and the team talk, with everyone sharing and getting to really know Jan for the first time. By the end of the meeting, they have cleared up a lot of their misunderstandings and really come to know each other as individuals rather than just coworkers. Although getting unstuck proves to be a difficult and emotional process, they all agree that having a more honest work environment and being able to honestly communicate with one another is well worth it.

MASTERING EMOTIONS AT WORK

But what happens when you're able to correctly identify these emotions but unable to properly express them, such as in an uptight office environment? People get stuck.

All emotions move through the same pipe, so to speak, so when one emotion is prevented from expression, the other four emotions get blocked as well.

Anger, sadness, etc., become trapped, growing exponentially with each passing day. Now, imagine a workplace full of these people—people who are denying their emotions, denying their very humanity, feeling stuck and unhappy, all in the name of professionalism. No wonder so many people are miserable at work!

When people get stuck, their emotions cannot stay bottled up inside of them forever. Eventually they need to find an outlet for release. Common releases include drinking, drugs, violence, shopping, etc. No wonder so many drivers are in the throes of road rage, or so many people abuse alcohol in their after-work hours! Their emotions are festering inside of them, leading them to become angry and scared individuals.

Who wants to work with someone like that? Who wants to *be* someone like that? No one, of course. And luckily you don't have to.

GETTING UNSTUCK

Here are some great ways that you and your office can get "unstuck" emotionally and start enjoying work again:

Start the timer!

In order to get unstuck, you need to first realize that emotions are not eternal, despite how interminable they often seem. If you allow yourself to feel an authentic emotion, it always moves through you in twenty seconds or less. No, really!

The reason that emotions usually fester for so long is because people won't allow themselves to truly feel what they are feeling. They may recognize it, and even give in to it for a few seconds, but generally people then shut it away, cap it off, and continue on with their business. For emotions like sadness, anger, and fear, it is easier to push the negative aside and address it later. But it's impossible for any good to come of that. By the time you do decide to address those emotions, they've moved so far beyond the realm of what they were originally that they are now practically unmanageable.

So the next time you feel sad, angry, etc., give yourself twenty seconds to feel it, and then try to move on. It might take some practice at first (after all, most of us are used to "feeling" an emotion for days at a time), but soon you will master the art of having your emotions in the office.

Accept your emotions

Mastering the art of authentic emoting begins with allowing yourself the right to feel whatever it is that you are feeling. Most of us grew up in a society in which we were told that some feelings were "good" (happiness, excitement, etc.) and some feelings were "bad" (sadness, fear, etc.). The end result is that most of us are uncomfortable feeling the "bad" emotions and spend most of our time chasing after the short-lived "good" emotions. However, the truth is that there is no good or bad in human emotion. How can an emotion be wrong? It would be like saying the weather is wrong. Yes, sometimes the weather isn't always comfortable or pleasant, but it certainly isn't wrong. Think of your emotions in the same way—it isn't pleasant to feel angry or sad, but it isn't wrong either. If you're feeling an emotion, you're feeling it. And that's just a basic fact.

Move your emotions

Now that you have accepted how you feel, you can act it out. By acting out your emotions, you can move them quickly through your system and make sure you don't get stuck. If you are sad, cry. If you are angry, scream or punch a pillow. If you are scared, shake for awhile and let yourself feel scared. To begin moving an emotion, start by acknowledging that it exists and that you are indeed feeling it. In my office I have set up a "bat station" with a firm round pillow and a baseball bat. Employees come to the bat station to take out their anger if these feelings arise during the day. By allowing themselves to really feel the anger and act it out, they are able to move the emotion through them. Thus, they are unfettered by their emotions and are better able to see possible solutions and creative ways to manage their current problem. Doesn't that seem so much more productive than stewing all day, pretending as if nothing is bothering you?

Cry in the office, if acceptable

Crying is a great release for pent-up emotions. If crying isn't acceptable in your office environment, then cry on your lunch break. It is healthy to regularly move your emotions, even if they are not bubbling up at that moment. Crying from time to time clears out the cobwebs of sadness you may build up during a week.

Tune in to your body

The body and the mind are intimately connected. Eastern medicine has realized this for centuries, but the Western world is just starting to understand the mind and body concept. When your emotional life is in distress, your physical body will feel the effects of it as well. That's why you may get a headache when you're feeling stressed, a stomachache if you're feeling nervous, or light-headedness if you're overwhelmed or excited. Research has shown that stress can make people more susceptible to colds and other ailments, while other studies have shown that positive thinking and meditation can help treat and reduce the negative effects of diseases such as cancer.

In short, when your frame of mind is healthy and fit, your body can be healthy and fit too—but when your mind is blocked, your body will become a testament to your inner distress. Some of the common ways the body responds to blocked emotions are back pain, upset stomach, and low energy.

Is it no wonder that offices are often havens for illnesses, back pain, upset stomachs, and yawning? Our emotional lives are not being cared for, and our physical bodies cannot help but be affected. Luckily, if employees simply free their emotions and allow them to be, they will notice their back pain, stomachaches, and lethargy all improve, if not totally disappear. As you begin enjoying the creation of a healthy frame of mind, you will feel better, sleep better, and yes...work better!

Watch yourself

Observe your own emotions as if you are outside of your body or head. You can have a dialogue running alongside your actual experience of the emotion. This allows you to feel and move your emotions without becoming your emotions. The dialogue in your head would go something like this: "I notice I am sad. I wonder what triggered that. I feel myself welling up and I am going to cry. Huh. Now it's subsiding. I notice it's gone." Once you have incorporated all of the techniques in this book, you may acquire a new perspective, a sort of running side dialogue of notice, exploration, and wonder. You may almost become a sort of narrator of your own existence. Don't worry; it doesn't mean you're nuts! It can be a very soothing and revealing dialogue. A second way of thinking. In fact, I am doing it right now as I write.

Manage sexual emotions

As you begin to accept the idea of emotions in the workplace, you are probably wondering where sexual feelings fit into this paradigm. After all, won't these lead to cases of sexual harassment and the like?

Actually, no. In fact, I believe that if people allowed themselves to accept their sexual feelings in the workplace, they wouldn't need to resort to secretive and corrupt behaviors such as harassment. We are human and our bodies are built to instinctively encompass sexual feelings, so turning these feelings off from nine to five is impossible and can sometimes backfire.

What's the alternative? You can realize the "sexiness" of a situation or a person and then retreat to a private moment in which you feel a little zing or say a little "woo-hoo!" inside your mind. Once you accept that those feelings are okay, they won't become stuck and fester away in the darkness. Think about how many relationships and reputations have been ruined because people simply can't accept that sexual feelings are okay! As long as you don't act on these feelings or behave inappropriately, feeling sexual attraction to a fellow coworker or employee is not a crime. Simply let it move through you (twenty seconds or less) and return to work. The object of your desire need never be the wiser.

Recognize your upper limits

Not only were most of us raised to view some emotions as negative and some emotions as positive, but we were also taught to cut off our emotions at a certain point. In other words, we learned to cap off our feelings whenever they become intense. This is even true when it comes to joy! Have you ever heard someone described as too happy? We think there must be something wrong with someone who is too happy. What is he, drunk? What is she, crazy? This is our upper limits coming into play. Whenever an emotion becomes too "big" and too real, we have to cut if off.

You probably do this much more than you realize. Have you ever found yourself looking for things to complain about, or looking for things to stress about? For instance, perhaps you are sitting home after a hard day at work and having dinner with your family. Sounds peaceful, right? A loving family, a nice home, warm food on the table—yet most of us can't relax and enjoy this moment. Our upper limits tell us we can't be this happy, this fortunate—so we look for things to stress about, like dirty laundry, the kids' homework, the snarky comment the boss made today. It seems hard to believe that any sane person would reject happiness, yet that is what most of us do every single day. Feeling pure happiness seems uncomfortable, as people generally thrive with a little bit of conflict. We want something to work toward, something to fix, something to overcome so that we may feel successful or like we've met a challenge. Happiness is such a pure and unbridled emotion that often we're not quite sure what to do with it. So we put it aside. Instead of creating those limits, recognize when you're placing limits on your emotions and then consciously try to live in the moment of your emotion. When you recognize the limitations you're imposing, and the rate at which you're placing them on yourself, you'll be able to manage your emotions more authentically. Then, when your upper limits go into effect, simply take note of it for what it is, and complete your emotion.

Recognize your own power

In chapter 2, the importance of owning your 100% was discussed. If you don't own your 100% of each situation, you will never be able to become unstuck of your own volition. You will require someone else to improve the situation before you will be able to move on. When you blame other people for your mood, you take away your own power to change or improve it. Yet who is responsible for your mood but you? You can blame your lazy coworkers or your rude boss, but in the end you are the only one who can decide whether or not to be an irritable ball of stress or a peaceful, productive employee. Taking responsibility for your own 100% can be one of the most empowering things you ever do—as it ultimately translates into taking responsibility for your life.

Call it out

If you notice that someone in your office (or in your personal life) is stuck in a certain drama or emotion, it might be helpful to communicate directly with the individual and share with them your observations. Ask your coworkers and friends to do the same for you. This is quite helpful because until you become more adept at recognizing authentic emotions and moving them, you might not realize when you are stuck. And certainly people recognize things far more in others than they ever do in themselves. Having someone bear witness to the fact that for the past three weeks you haven't stopped agonizing over missing a promotion might help you to realize when you are stuck, and you can return the favor when the opportunity arises.

Use this tip judiciously. No one likes a know-it-all, and most of what you spot is probably true for yourself (see "You Spot It, You Got It" in chapter 10). Similarly, when those in your life point out that you are stuck, welcome their observation.

Calling it out for yourself

What's important is that you need to have enough of an awareness of yourself that you are able to notice when *you're* getting stuck. It's okay to be stuck; it's just important that you recognize when you get stuck and why you get stuck and in what situations you communicate the most inauthentically. Once you are aware of these traits within yourself, then you will be able to call yourself to consciousness about being stuck, as well as to respond positively to those who call it to your attention. To help yourself not get stuck in the workplace, it's important to regularly come clean with your colleagues and make sure you don't let any negative emotions build up to an unmanageable point. If you work consciously on achieving those things, both for yourself and your relationships with your colleagues, then you will be in a great place to ensure that you remain as unstuck as possible.

Also, it's important to note the persona to which you most often resort. Are you communicating with everyone authentically? Or are you stuck unless you are conducting yourself via one specific persona? Also, check the language you're using. When you're working, does the language you use with your coworkers and clients line up with positive, forward thinking? If not, then that is a strong signal for what might be getting you stuck. Part of remaining unstuck is thinking in a way that always moves you forward. If you're thinking negatively about the past, or negatively in general, then you're engaging in a frame of thought that solely promotes being stuck because it doesn't allow you to think authentically.

BECOME THE MASTER OF YOUR EMOTIONS

Becoming unstuck means taking charge of your emotional life. In your life you are meant to be the driver, not the passenger. The key thing to remember is that you are ultimately the one in charge of your emotional life; no matter how others seem to be affecting your emotional happiness or unhappiness, the power to control your emotions in the best way possible is completely in your hands. Emotions are not meant to buffet us to and fro and leave us helpless in their wake. Emotions are meant to enrich our lives, engender our creativity, and engage our empathy. Without emotions our lives would be completely devoid of color, but that doesn't mean we can't be in control of the picture they ultimately paint.

It is possible to decide what kind of day you are going to have at the office and the type of relationships you will have with your colleagues—all you have to do is decide whether you will be the master of your emotions or a slave to them.

- When you don't communicate authentically, emotions get stuck inside of you. When you are stuck, your creativity, happiness, and productivity get blocked.
- In order to get unstuck, you need to vocalize your emotions and thoughts authentically with those around you.
- You can keep from getting stuck by regularly practicing authentic communication.

CHAPTER 5

IT'S A GIFT

THE ROLE OF NEGATIVE FEEDBACK

Excellence is the unlimited ability to improve the quality of what you have to offer.

—Rick Pitino

As I'm sure you've experienced, nothing can create a bad day quite like negative feedback from your boss or your colleagues. However, a working environment where no challenges are addressed would not be a very productive one. Indeed, negative feedback is actually necessary for the creation of a healthy work environment and a team of productive employees. You could even say that negative feedback is a gift. But to ensure that it is received like a gift, you have to make sure you are delivering and receiving this feedback appropriately.

Office Scene: Giving Negative Feedback
The Scene: Carter and Rosen, a law firm

The Problem: Not knowing how to accept negative feedback

The People: Sarah (the executive administrative assistant), Heather (an administrative assistant), Maria (a coworker)

Sarah has been an employee at Carter and Rosen, a law firm, for over twenty years, working her way up from a mailroom secretary to executive administrative assistant. Throughout her tenure at Carter and Rosen, Sarah worked extremely hard, devoting herself to the company unendingly. She knew that if she proved herself and her dedication to the company, it would pay off in the long term and she would reap the benefits of her loyalty and strong work ethic. Because of all this, Sarah prides herself on her hard work and dedicated enthusiasm, which prompts the higher-ups to entrust her with the highly important task of compiling the company's annual report.

With the report's due date approaching fast, Sarah begins to realize that to finish the report successfully she'll need another person to help her complete the project. After meeting with her boss to make sure this won't be an issue, her boss assigns Heather, a new administrative assistant, to the task. Sarah takes it upon herself to show Heather the ropes, introducing her to the higher-ups and giving her as much information about Carter and Rosen as possible.

At first Heather seems confused by the work Sarah has given her to do. She doesn't have much experience in the field, and, only being an administrative assistant, it seems to take her a long time to catch on to instructions. She's not generating material for the report at the rate Sarah hoped she would, and after awhile Sarah suspects that she's not getting any of the work assigned to her done at all. On top of it all, Heather even begins showing up late to their early morning project meetings.

At first Sarah is not sure how to handle the situation. She tries to remain friendly but makes sure she mentions to Heather several times that deadlines and meetings are extremely important, hoping Heather will understand that she needs to adjust her work habits so that they can finish the report on time.

Then Heather begins to miss the project meetings altogether, always giving an excuse about why she couldn't make it. Sarah begins to get angry with her coworker and frustrated with her complete lack of interest in finishing the reports. When Sarah was an administrative assistant, she would have been thrilled with the opportunity to work on such a prestigious report, but Heather seems to approach her responsibilities with a complete lack of regard for the task at hand. Finally, instead of explaining to Heather what she has to do to improve her performance, Sarah starts to think it would just be easier to do all the work on her own. She starts pushing Heather off of the project, taking over tasks she had originally assigned to her.

But eventually the work starts to pile up again, and Sarah becomes extremely scared. She misses her first draft deadline and asks her boss for more time. Her coworkers begin to notice that she is missing lunch; after she comes in late to work after working late the night before, one of her coworkers confronts her.

"I think you have blown this way out of proportion, Sarah," says Maria after Sarah explains the situation and Heather's failings as an assistant to her. "Have you actually sat down and spoken with Heather about the problems you are having and why she seems so unresponsive?"

"I already told her that our meetings and deadlines are vital to finishing the report on time. Other than that, I don't know what to do. I don't know why she can't just understand the importance of the project in the first place and do everything she can to make sure she gets her tasks completed on time." Sarah sighs, a feeling of helplessness overwhelming her. "I'm not her boss! Who am I to criticize her and the awful job she is doing?"

"Look, Heather is new here, and she doesn't have a lot of experience," explains Maria. "Maybe she doesn't fully understand the function of the report, or perhaps she hasn't realized how her actions are affecting you and the project. I think any feedback you can give her would be a gift, not a criticism. The best thing you could do for her is to be patient and continue to explain things to her so that you can help her grow as an employee and as a person."

At first Sarah isn't convinced. Why should she present a "gift" to Heather when she has made her job so much harder? If Heather hasn't been able to handle the work, why should Sarah compromise all of her hard work and dedication just to help Heather learn the company's ropes?

The next morning Sarah flips on her computer only to find that Heather has yet again managed to disorganize the files, adding an hour to Sarah's workload. This is the last straw for Sarah, and she marches over to Heather's desk. "I've been feeling that you don't take this project as seriously as I do," says Sarah. "You've continuously missed important meetings and deadlines, and on top of that you constantly disorganize my work—I don't understand it! I know you are new, and I've offered to sit down and explain things, but you always tell me you don't need any help. Please tell me what I can do to help you complete your tasks efficiently and get everything done on time."

Heather turns red and immediately starts to fidget, showing a great amount of discomfort. "I don't know, Sarah. You say you'll help me, but that's only after you've become frustrated with my work," explains Heather. "You never gave me a chance to learn anything. I know you have a lot of experience in this field, but I don't, and I need direction. Furthermore, when something isn't done correctly, it would be helpful to know where I went wrong rather than to just get yelled at. I can't fix anything for the future if I don't know what wasn't working initially."

Sarah is speechless. She always considered herself to be an easygoing and friendly person. How could Heather have misunderstood that? She must be mistaken! But as Sarah's frustration begins to bubble up, Maria's words suddenly make sense. Instead of becoming defensive, Sarah sees Heather's feedback as a gift, giving her a candid picture of herself. She can now take this information and use it to become a better coworker, project supervisor, and, one day, boss.

"Thank you for being honest with me," says Sarah, a smile spreading across her face. "I promise that from here on out, I will work with you rather than against you. I'm really sorry, Heather; I didn't realize that I was being such a poor communicator and frustrating supervisor. I really appreciate your honesty and feedback, and I think that because of this conversation we've both received an invaluable gift. I hope you still want to continue working with me."

"Of course," Heather replies graciously. "Thanks for taking my feedback to heart, and I'm really looking forward to working with you now and learning more about the job and how Carter and Rosen works."

"Excellent!" Sarah is glad to have cleared up this misunderstanding. "Let's get started!"

DELIVERING NEGATIVE FEEDBACK

It's inevitable that a situation will arise in which you must give someone in your office negative feedback. If someone broaches an idea in a meeting that you know is misguided, it would be a disservice to your company and to your coworker not to let her know that her idea won't fly. However, the way you deliver this message will determine whether or not the message is a gift or criticism.

> A message that is feedback will have actionable information, while a message that is a criticism will simply be derogatory. Feedback is a gift.

For example, a typical response to a bad idea launched in a meeting might simply be scorn, or a statement like "No way! That won't work. Don't you remember what happened last time when we tried something similar? Moving on!" Meanwhile, the person who brought up the idea has no clue how she can improve in the future and also most likely feels attacked and even angry at how she was treated.

Negative feedback that is a gift would include helpful information such as, "That idea doesn't take into consideration the logistics problem we encountered last time. Let's try to focus our efforts on an action plan that won't involve that specific vendor." Not only will this spur the brainstorm meeting in the right direction, but it will also help employees continue to feel valued, even when their ideas aren't on point.

A workplace where employees don't feel safe making mistakes or trying something new is a workplace where creativity and ingenuity will not thrive. Criticism and degradation are useless in the workplace, but guided, honest feedback is completely useful. Here are a few examples of negative feedback that is a gift:

- ✓ This project you turned in has numerous spelling errors. (The employee can improve her work and hence become better at her job and more qualified.)
- ✓ You were late five times this month. (The employee will learn punctuality and that employers will not tolerate lateness.)
- ✓ The client is angry that you missed her deadline. (The employee will know that the client is not pleased with her and that time commitments are important.)
- ✓ You don't share the workload on projects. (The employee will learn that she needs to brush up on her teamwork skills.)

All of the above statements will no doubt be jarring and even upsetting for the person to hear at first. No employee likes to hear that their work is poor. But if the employee accepts the feedback in the spirit in which it is intended, she will be able to improve and fine-tune her performance in the future.

This brings us to the most difficult part—learning to accept negative feedback.

RECEIVING NEGATIVE FEEDBACK

It is very easy to accept feedback that bolsters our sense of self (in other words, it is very easy to accept praise). However, it is not so easy to accept feedback that seems to attack or downgrade us. We don't want to hear that our work has spelling errors, that we aren't being a team player, or that our project idea isn't fresh. Though these are minor statements, they seem to carry much more sinister messages, such as: *You're careless, you're selfish, you're not creative, and you are useless to this team.* Eek! No wonder people hate to hear even the slightest negative feedback in the office.

Most of us never learned how to take negative feedback correctly. We wrongly assume that anything that is less than positive feedback is meant to attack who we are and denigrate us. We build a wall around ourselves that is meant to protect us from any negativity, out of fear that we might hear something truly awful about ourselves. Why else would it be so upsetting when someone suggests your work would benefit from a slight improvement?

> Learning to accept negative feedback begins with opening ourselves to the truth that the world isn't the enemy.

By accepting (even just slightly) that everyone has something valuable they can teach us about who we are, we open up to a realm of creativity, growth, and success that we never thought possible. This means accepting negative feedback with an open mind and discovering what you must do to improve your performance.

This will take some practice. It is our natural reaction to immediately leap to our own defense whenever someone puts us down. We immediately come up with several different rebuttals, all of which are aimed at preventing us from taking a single iota of responsibility for the situation at hand. However, if you can take a step back, a deep breath, and remove yourself from the situation for a moment, you might realize you are being told something worthwhile, something that can help you grow personally and professionally.

The times when you struggle the most to accept negative feedback or even momentarily remove your defenses are the times when you have the most to learn. This is especially true if someone comes at you angrily with feedback.

> Any time that someone has a lot of negative energy concerning you or your job performance is a time when you have plenty to learn.

If you have sparked that much emotion in someone, there is something happening that needs to be addressed—not deflected or defended.

This is not to say you don't have the right to get upset whenever you hear negative feedback. It is perfectly natural to feel sad, angry, or any variation thereof when you hear that your performance needs work. Allow yourself to feel those emotions, but don't allow yourself to become them. Otherwise, you will be so busy being angry or sad that you won't have the emotional energy or wherewithal to realize where you stand to improve.

WONDER MOMENTS

After enough practice at accepting negative feedback, you might even come across a "wonder moment." A "wonder moment" is when you are so open to the world that you almost immediately realize the truth in a bit of negative feedback. An involuntary "hmm!" noise might even come out of you as you realize something you need to improve upon, such as: "Wow! Scott is right; I did make the client wait for me for over thirty minutes. I really do need to manage my time better." Or, "There is a big error in my TPS report. Next time I will double-check before I send it off."

One useful tactic that may help you take negative feedback in stride and reach a wonder moment involves a physical gesture called "scooping." Bring your arms to the top of your head, then reach out in front of you, and pull your arms back toward you. This large "scooping" motion will help remind you that you need to let the world in, whether it is giving you negative feedback or positive feedback. Not everything you hear will be useful or true, but if you approach feedback openly, you will hear valuable and life-changing truths throughout your career.

Office Scene: The Wrong Way to Build Morale

The Scene: Imaging Consults, Inc.

The Problem: Criticism never works

The People: Kerri (the president), Nicholas (the CEO)

Kerri is the president of Imaging Consults, Inc. For the last year her primary goal has been to whip her staff into shape in order to increase the company's quickly decreasing sales numbers, but all she gets is resistance. While in meetings, her staff is listless, insubordinate, and unwilling to take initiative. They seem uninterested in the problem, uninterested in stepping up their individual responsibilities to increase sales, and uninterested in Kerri's leadership and determination. Because of this, the meetings often end with her yelling at one or all of them to shape up their sales numbers and start producing. She generally ends up leaving the meetings in a huff, her staff unmotivated and frustrated.

Despite all of this, every Monday Kerri comes into the office and the numbers are still the same. In fact, the only thing that has changed in the past year is that Imaging Consults' employee satisfaction has dropped even lower than it was when she first started. Between this and the lack of progress in the sales department, she knows that something seriously needs to change. After another frustrating and unsuccessful company meeting, she sits down with the CEO of her company, Nicholas, explains to him the problem, and asks what he thinks she should do.

"You need to get the numbers up! That's what you need to do!" he snaps. "Quit mollycoddling the employees. We trusted you as president of the company to take charge of the employees and create results. You said you can handle this job—but now it seems you can't. Maybe it was a mistake to have hired you. Imaging Consults hasn't made any progress since you've been hired, and I'm sick of looking at weekly progress reports reflecting no progress. You are awful at this."

Kerri leaves his office dejected and deflated and still not knowing what to do, but she really isn't all that surprised. Nicholas always lashes out at people like this. He is notorious for calling people into his office and screaming at them and declaring them incompetent whenever something isn't functioning exactly the way he wants it to. At this point Kerri doesn't even know why she thought Nicholas would help; he has yelled at her more times than she could count. Why doesn't Nicholas realize that when people approach him with problems or need his advice, his anger is useless at helping to motivate his staff? If he really wants to supervise and guide his employees, he'd realize that working with them to achieve a solution is a lot more effective than yelling at them and telling them they're worthless.

Suddenly Kerri groans and hangs her head. She realizes that when she is trying to motivate and encourage her employees to increase their sales, she is really only treating them in the same demeaning way that Nicholas treats her. After she thinks about it she realizes that of course their numbers aren't going to go up—her yelling at them to do their jobs better every week isn't any more useful than the demotivating tongue-lashing she just received from Nicholas. She decides that from now on she will focus more on her criticism and making it less abrasive—if it isn't useful, she won't say it. Rather, she will take more consideration in how she addresses her employees, making sure to communicate with them rather than against them.

The next Monday, when Kerri implements her new ideas on criticism, it results in her staff meeting running much differently and far more positively. When her employees speak, she doesn't arbitrarily shoot down their ideas or snap at people who approach her with mistakes they have made. Instead she makes sure that when she is discussing an issue with her staff, she offers thoughtful guidance and encouraging solutions. When someone confesses to losing another account, she inquires why it happened instead of initially resorting to angry backlash. After her employee explains to her that it is because the client found a cheaper firm, she realizes that the loss of this account was completely outside of her employee's control. Once she is able to let this resonate—that not every account loss is due to an employee's lack of care or concern for their job—she reminds herself not to lose her temper at the employee and instead says, "Well, that's out of your control. You don't determine price. Let's not cry over spilled accounts. Let's just focus on getting an even better account in the future."

After the meeting the entire mood of the room is completely different from normal. Everyone wonders why Kerri is in such a good mood, but assumes it is a fluke of some sort and does not expect this kind of positive behavior during every meeting. However, after a month of her new demeanor, the spirit of the office starts to lift. People quit dreading coming to work for the weekly meetings, and a few even start looking forward to working with the company as a team to brainstorm new business ideas every Monday.

Within three months, Imaging Consults earns itself ten new accounts, a new account record unheard of before in the firm. When Nicholas asks Kerri how she managed to pull it off, she says smilingly, "After being yelled at by you so many times, I realized how awful it felt, and that that was exactly how my staff felt. So I decided to only offer negative feedback if I knew it would be constructive in some way. Even then I vowed to make my negative feedback something more positive so that my employees wouldn't feel berated by me constantly."

Nicholas takes the hint and soon begins to readjust his approach to feedback in the office. Soon the entire company is imbued with a different work ethic and everyone feels motivated to work together to make the company the best it can be.

- There is a right way and a wrong way to offer negative feedback. When you offer negative feedback the wrong way, employees or coworkers have no way to change their behavior. When you offer feedback the right way, they will know and understand what needs to change.
- Negative feedback is what helps people to grow and improve. When someone offers you negative feedback, consider it a gift and use it to your advantage.

CHAPTER 6

PROFIT BY APPRECIATION

THE ROLE OF POSITIVE FEEDBACK

By appreciation, we make excellence in others our own property.

—Voltaire

Positive feedback is even more crucial in the workplace than negative feedback. While negative feedback has the power to help employees grow and improve their performance, positive feedback has the power to help people stay motivated and inspired.

Many corporations realize the importance of appreciation in the office, but their efforts to appreciate and commend their staff usually come in the traditional form of Christmas bonuses, casual Fridays, swanky offices, and the like. However, these impersonal and large-scale rewards for the company do very little in the way of making each employee feel valued as an individual and as a talented team member.

They quickly become expected parts of an employee's compensation package.

The only true way to show your employees or coworkers appreciation is through positive feedback.

Office Scene: A Tale of Two Appreciations

The Scene: Scion, Inc.

The Problem: Not appreciating your coworkers

The People: Claire (a publicist), Brenda (a publicist), Jake (the boss)

Claire and Brenda are both publicists with Scion, Inc., working on the account of a notable plastic surgeon. They've been working together as publicists on this account for the past six months, and it's one of the biggest and most widely known clients their public relations company has. For the last six months, they have both been working overtime to pull in top media hits and have been very successful in gaining national attention for both the client and their PR firm. Their client couldn't be any happier with the excellent representation the company is receiving, and their boss, Jake, is excited by their progress. However, despite the success of their hard work, Claire and Brenda can't seem to stop butting heads.

Claire's specialty is in landing print placements as opposed to television or radio. She's had great success in landing mentions in multiple national news publications in newspapers, print journals, and magazines. Yet she's frustrated because she feels that Brenda overshadows her success by overtly and aggressively bragging about her television placements. Even though top television shows garner more media impressions than print placements, Claire knows that print media is just as crucial to a client's success. After all, the surgeon's lobby is now decorated with many of his high-profile newspaper placements. But despite their partnership, Brenda always claims credit for the bulk of their client's success, claiming that television hits are where the real impressions are made.

After weeks of cold silences and petty arguments, Claire is at the end of her rope. She wants Brenda to appreciate her and to recognize the importance of her contributions to their partnership. Confused about how to approach such a touchy situation, Claire sits down to really analyze the events of the past six months so that she can clearly and honestly articulate to Brenda why she feels so slighted. As she thinks about the way they interact, she comes to an uncomfortable realization. Here she is, lamenting the fact that Brenda isn't appreciating her when she hasn't at all tried to appreciate Brenda and the hard work she has put into their account. She realizes then she has spent so much effort trying to get her own performance and newspaper hits praised that she hasn't bothered to give any thought and praise to Brenda's hard work. Indeed, the more Brenda is able to get their client publicized on television, the easier Claire's job is at placing him in major printed publications.

Claire decides that their hard work could be much more effective if the two of them can just stop squabbling and learn to be more conscious of appreciating each other's contributions. She makes a spreadsheet that tracks all the media hits their client has received in the last six months, with a special emphasis on the many great television hits Brenda has received. She even attaches a special memo to the spreadsheet applauding her efforts.

When Brenda sees what Claire has done, she is shocked by Claire's outburst of kindness. Seeing the effort Claire has made to give acknowldgment to her hard work makes her realize that she has been really unappreciative of all the work Claire has contributed. After all, any media they get for their client is great for both of them and the company, no matter where it lands. Once Jake sees how Brenda and Claire worked together to rectify their situation, he is incredibly impressed by their maturity and professionalism. So impressed, in fact, that he gives them both a raise—and another client to work on together!

GIVING POSITIVE FEEDBACK

I was first taught the importance of appreciation when my life coach explained to me this concept:

> The best way to get appreciation from someone is to give it.

Her reciprocal attitude about appreciation really resonated with me, and I vowed to be more conscious of instituting that with my own employees.

I witnessed the importance of individual and specific appreciation when I began approving pitches that my team wrote for their clients. (At Empower we pitch our clients to the media weekly, so every week I receive a batch of short, creative, sexy pitches that I then approve for content and messaging.) When I respond to these pitches, I say one of the following if I approve the pitch: "Good work," "I love it!" or "Okay" (this last response being the least enthusiastic). Over time I noticed that when an employee got a couple of "okay" responses instead of the "I love it!" appreciation, her work the next week would be improved. Why? Not because there is anything negative in the "send it out" response, but because people crave positive appreciation for their work. And not just any type of bland, general appreciation—they want enthusiastic, individual praise like an "I love it!" response. The boost that an employee gets from such a response fosters a positive reaction that rivals even that of a raise. (People always love more money, but that doesn't mean praise and appreciation are outdated.)

After discovering how useful my short email appreciations were, I realized I had come across a gold mine of opportunity. If I appreciated my employees every day, and perhaps even got them to appreciate each other, I would have a work environment that hummed with creativity and inspiration.

But how could I implement appreciations in a way that felt alive and valid? I decided to start every staff meeting with an "appreciation toss" in which my employees and I toss a small beanbag around the room. With each toss, the person tossing the bag shares an appreciation with the person to whom the bag is tossed. Once I got the beanbag rolling, my team easily got the hang of it, sharing appreciations such as:

- *I appreciate the way you always keep me laughing, even when I am so stressed.*
- *I appreciate how you are always so helpful on projects.*
- *I appreciate your positive attitude.*
- *I appreciate that you always make coffee in the morning!*

Whether the appreciation is big or small, humorous or serious, tossing the beanbag around is hugely beneficial. The only caveat is to make the appreciation as specific and individual as possible.

Not only does a climate of appreciation allow everyone to feel liked and part of the team, but it also teaches them how to share with one another and learn to respect and admire their colleagues.

> Camaraderie can't be forced on employees through corporate training or "trust" exercises, but it can be created organically through appreciation and mutual respect.

Sharing appreciations can also help people learn how to get along with coworkers with whom they might not have gotten along in the past. A good practice to implement is to encourage employees to find three things to appreciate about someone they are not getting along with. They don't necessarily have to share these three appreciations with the person (unless they want to). Just thinking these three appreciations is enough to improve their frame of mind and get them in the habit of seeing their coworkers in a positive light, even when they are not getting along. Instead of seeing only the perceived negative aspects of their colleagues (i.e., *she doesn't do her share of work* or *he is an attention seeker*), they will force their minds to create a new script by thinking things like *she has a good sense of humor* or *he is really great at making spreadsheets*. These positive appreciations might not completely replace the issue they are concerned with, but they will help them to realize that their coworker isn't pure evil.

FRIENDSHIP IN THE WORKPLACE

Real, enjoyable friendships are a rarity in the workplace. Coworkers too often view each other as competition for raises and promotions, and after spending every workday together for months at a time, they began to grate on each other's nerves. For instance, one employee can't stand the way his office mate snaps his gum, another employee is sick of the way his coworker always polishes off the last of the coffee without making more, and another person hates the sound of his colleague's iTunes. Although all of these annoyances are petty, they can often grow into a hailstorm in the confined and tense atmosphere of traditional corporate environments.

But what if these people, what if *you*, were able to view the people you work with as friends? As people to celebrate victories with, cry over disappointments with, and work alongside happily? Sounds too good to be true, right?

Not if you create an environment of appreciation and mutual respect in your office. Grasping for praise or the next bonus leads coworkers to look at each other as obstacles rather than helping hands. Sharing appreciations and learning how to look on one another as teammates creates trust, admiration, and even friendship.

Despite what traditional corporate wisdom tells us, there is a place for friendships and appropriate personal relationships within the workplace. Friendships and a friendly environment contribute to the mental and physical health of every employee, which lowers insurance claims, reduces depression, improves workplace attendance, and promotes employee loyalty. When employees know they are going into work every day in an office where they are respected, loved, and supported, they will have a completely different experience than employees who come into the workplace feeling like their coworkers are aggressive, rude, or derogatory. This difference is made evident in the work they do and the amount of time they remain at a company.

BANISHING ENTITLEMENT

Entitlement is a mask for anger, and it is always born out of a persona. Many of us have a persona that feels enraged or hurt when the world is not "fair" or "just." This is generally an emotional place in which many people get stuck. Shifting entitlement into appreciation is an emotional somersault, because the two are polar opposites.

Entitlement is a common problem in corporate environments, mainly because people feel like they are "owed" certain rewards. For example, picture a company outing that requires employees to stay overnight at a hotel. Even though the hotel is a decent establishment, the employees find plenty to complain about. One employee doesn't like the minibar options, one employee doesn't like the sweetener by the coffee machines, and one employee is angry that her wake-up call was late. Despite the fact that these are minor issues, the employees harp about it and only focus on what went wrong during their stay, forgetting to even thank their employer for buying them a nice dinner.

One way to shift the focus of this entitled, complaining group of employees is to host a morning appreciation meeting. As ideas are exchanged and appreciations come up, people will be surprised to notice all of the little nice things they didn't notice before, like the mints on the table or the cinnamon buns in the conference room.

The next time you feel angry or sad about something, ask if this emotion is a result of an entitlement persona. For example, are you really angry about having to work late, or are you angry you have to work late because you think it is "not fair"? Search for these little entitlement moments as they pop up in your life, and try to vanquish them by searching for appreciations to replace those complaints.

MORE VALUABLE THAN MONEY

Appreciations, and the positive energy that springs out of them, are more valuable than money. From an employer's perspective, anything that keeps employees happy, healthy, and coming to work every day with a positive attitude means more than anything else. From an employee's perspective, the knowledge that you work at a place where appreciations and friendship abound is more powerful and appealing than the knowledge that there are Christmas bonuses or year-end raises.

Employees and employers are not the only people who benefit from an appreciative work environment. Appreciations can also extend to your business dealings with clients as well. At my public relations firm we regularly send our clients letters of appreciation, generally about four a year. These letters, in conjunction with routine positive communication from us every week, keep them feeling understood, valued, and part of our firm. We also use these letters of appreciation to promote new business opportunities, by mailing out personalized and meaningful letters or emails to potential new clients.

Client appreciations also have their place behind the scenes, when they are not even there to hear the good things said about them. Whenever I lead a staff meeting and we are discussing clients, I always ask the account executives to first share an appreciation about their client before we begin to discuss strategy on the account. I find that this promotes creativity and inspiration in the room and clears away any stress or negativity that the account executive might be feeling toward his or her client. After all, if we don't appreciate our clients, we can't expect the rest of the world to do so!

- Positive feedback encourages growth, productivity, and a happy, healthy work environment.
- If you want positive feedback, you have to give it. Often when we feel the most unappreciated, it is because we are not putting out the positive feedback we so desperately want.
- Implement positive feedback in your office by having an appreciation toss before meetings or during lunch.
- Make it a rule that every request or complaint is followed or preceded by an appreciation of some sort, in order to keep the office environment from becoming negative or toxic.

CHAPTER 7

SPEAKING UNARGUABLY

LEAVING MISUNDERSTANDINGS IN THE DUST

The single biggest problem in communication is the illusion that it has taken place.

—George Bernard Shaw

Most of us withhold our true thoughts and feelings from the people in our lives. When we communicate with one another, there's a certain amount of mental editing that occurs before we actually say what we say. We run certain questions through our head: "Will it offend them if I say this?"; "I don't want them to think I'm being too emotional"; "I won't say it like that, they'll think I'm rude," etc. Very rarely do people share how they really, honestly feel with one another. Such reticence is usually excused by the idea of "good manners." After all, no one wants to cause a scene or offend someone or hurt their feelings. So we keep to the pleasantries of life and say only the things that are certain not to offend.

This is especially true in office life, where social and communicative interaction is on a heightened, formal level. We hold our coworkers and our clients at an arm's length and resist sharing any real part of ourselves.

This all seems somewhat antithetical, as this aloof and cold style of communication doesn't come naturally in human relationships. Generally, human relationships are marked by a desire to communicate, to share, to open up. The people with whom we surround ourselves have like-minded interests that stimulate discussion and the sharing of opinions and thoughts. Although you may not care for *everyone* working in your office, you obviously share things in common with some of the people with whom you work, otherwise you wouldn't have all pursued a similar field.

Thus, it seems silly to restrict authentic communication with your coworkers, especially considering the amount of time most individuals spend at work. No wonder so many people get drunk at office holiday parties and make fools of themselves! After spending the whole year wrapped in a cold, distant persona, keeping their true selves from those around them, they leap at the chance to let loose and be real. It's just a shame that this kind of fun, heartened interaction can only occur once a year, and with the aid of beverages, to boot!

Is it possible to bring our real, authentic selves into the office? Can we address issues as they arise rather than keeping up an impersonal and distant demeanor? Can we let people know when they hurt our feelings or make us angry without fears of repercussions? Yes, we can—through "completing" with one another in an environment of open, honest communication.

Office Scene: The "Perfect" Team

The Scene: The Computer Den, a computer company

The Problem: Arguing in circles

The People: Mark (a salesperson), Linda (a supervisor), Kara (a salesperson)

Mark is a salesperson for the Computer Den. He is very talented at his job, and he loves landing new accounts for his firm. However, his supervisor, Linda, recently partnered him up with another salesperson, Kara, with whom he does not get along. The two coworkers butt heads over everything, from splitting up tasks to where to eat for lunch. Things finally reach a breaking point when the two end up quarreling in front of a potential client, and Linda decides that it is time for her to intervene.

Linda brings Mark and Kara into her office to get to the root of their difficulties. When pressed, Kara admits that she finds some of Mark's work habits to be very frustrating and at times even infuriating. For example, Kara explains, she hates that Mark always procrastinates and that he doesn't act professionally in meetings. "How so?" splutters Mark. Kara illustrates by mentioning a few times when Mark acted too friendly and open with clients, at least in her opinion.

"You're right—that is your opinion," says Mark. "And I happen to think that my clients like being treated like friends. They certainly don't enjoy the cold shoulder you give them." Mark continues, "As for my 'procrastinating,' I think I call that having a social life. Yes, I don't stay till eight o' clock every night. But that's because I have things to do. If you don't, that's your problem. And guess what else? I am sick of your late-night phone calls and early morning wake-up calls. Leave me alone after I leave the office—I am sick of you ruining my time off with your nasty attitude."

"Ooohhh, now I have a nasty attitude when I call you?" asks Kara. "You're the jerk who leaves me to do all the work—what do you want me to do, thank you for that?"

"Stop!" shouts Linda. "Enough! Do you guys remember last summer when we went to the team-building meeting and learned to speak unarguably? By sourcing a thought, a physical sensation, or the pure facts? Let's try to do that now. No more name-calling and story-telling."

"Fine," says Kara. "Mark, when you leave work unfinished, I feel sick to my stomach if I don't finish it for you. I don't like leaving the office with our tasks undone."

"I understand that," Mark replies. "But I think that I deserve a balance between work and my personal life.

I stay late some nights, but I can't commit to that every night. I do my share of the work—I just don't do it at a breakneck pace."

"What about the Tinley account?" asks Kara. "In that situation you left early for the holidays and I had to cover for you. I would have liked to leave early too, but I had to make sure the client received the products he was promised," says Kara, sourcing the facts.

Silent for a moment, Mark nods and says, "That's true. I did leave you hanging that one time. But that was months ago. Since then I think I have been a good team player. I just want you to understand that when you call me late at night about work, it stresses me out and makes me feel angry. I want to enjoy my time off, and I can't do it if you call me and ream me out at nine o' clock at night."

Kara considers his point. "I can agree not to call you after hours anymore if you can agree to make sure that we each meet our deadlines every week. On special occasions I am willing to cover for you—but I want you to do the same for me. I have a wedding coming up in two weeks, and I would like to leave the office with the knowledge that you won't leave the work undone."

"Agreed," says Mark. "And have fun at your wedding. Don't worry about a thing."

"Maybe we do make the perfect team, after all!" jokes Kara.

THE POWER OF COMPLETING

What does it mean to "complete" with someone?

> Completing is when you share your untold thoughts and give voice to the hidden stories and beliefs in your head.

When you don't share what is true for you, you are not being authentic. You are projecting a false or incomplete story into the workplace. Thus, when you do communicate authentically and share your hidden emotions and stories, you are "completing" the communication loop. For example, if you want to complete with your coworker about her poor work ethic, you might say, "Christine, you are a lot of fun to work with, but I think that lately you haven't been pulling your weight." You might find out that Christine isn't being lazy but is instead dealing with health issues that the boss is well aware of—so rather than being secretly annoyed with her for weeks, you give her the understanding and compassion she needs.

Such frank and forthright communication sounds counterproductive to a healthy work environment—after all, who wants to hear that they are not pulling their weight? But the truth is that honesty is always necessary for healthy communication. In fact, in a healthy work environment people are completing with each other all the time!

That's right. The best way to create a healthy and harmonious work environment is to consistently complete with your coworkers. It is the only way to clear out the tension and unspoken resentments that can hold us back and stifle our happiness and creativity. The more you complete with the people in your life, the less anxiety and distress you will feel.

One of the most dangerous repercussions of not completing with someone is the buildup of resentment that develops when your true emotions about something are not shared. Something as simple as the annoyance you feel when your office mate pops their gum can build up over time until your anger has escalated excessively beyond the initial problem. Resentment is easy to harbor and it can become all-consuming unless it is checked and released as soon as it's begun.

Once you complete with your coworkers about those ticks and habits that bother you, your frame of mind and your emotions will be clean and ready to receive positive energy. And by nipping things in the bud immediately, you can prevent any "big" completions from being necessary. Instead you will only have to share smaller, less potent completions, as you will never allow negative emotions to stew inside of you.

However, it isn't just negative emotions that people can complete with each other.

Positive emotions are even more important than negative emotions for completing.

Unsaid appreciations can build up and cause regret in the person who does not express them, much in the same way that people regret all their unsaid "I love you's" after someone close to them dies. Yes, that person probably knew that you loved them without your having to say it, but hearing and saying those words are part of the beauty of being human. Plus, what better way to increase positive, authentic communication in the office than to positively complete with your coworkers?

Many people feel positive emotions toward others without ever expressing them. Perhaps you really enjoy working with one of your coworkers because they're such a good teammate, or you appreciate that one of your employees always has a positive attitude and a smile on their face. Even if it's as simple as you like your staff member's taste in clothing, or you enjoy the good conversation you two have over lunch, completing these positive emotions rather than keeping them inside stimulates a much more positive interoffice environment and communicates to your colleagues that you value them as individuals just as much as coworkers. Plus, who doesn't enjoy random positive compliments throughout the day?

> Some of the best compliments are those that are unasked for and given without a specific reason—true authenticity.

Appreciating a colleague quietly is not as valuable as sharing this appreciation with him or her out loud. Indeed, there is already so much negativity in the world and in the workplace that even the slightest glimmer of appreciation can modify someone's entire outlook, yet many people still withhold these powerful and moving words.

Why? Those who are afraid to speak their minds truthfully and keep to themselves, hidden in their office, can appear rude, stuck-up, unwilling to socialize and communicate. And more often than not, that's not the case. It just goes to show that you really have nothing to lose by completing and being as open as possible. You can't get along with "too many" of your coworkers. And if work is a place where you spend the majority of your time, you can't have "too many" coworkers whom you also consider friends.

So why do people choose to withhold the powerful, impacting thoughts that run through their minds? Perhaps you grew up in a household where emotions were hidden and never shared, or perhaps you feel awkward or unused to complimenting the people in your life, especially those you work with.

However, sharing appreciations and positive feedback is actually one of the easiest things to do in the world. And like all things new and different, you may feel slightly awkward or uneasy with communicating and completing in ways you're not used to. But you don't have to be a charmer or a wordsmith to offer a great compliment; you just have to be someone who's willing to tell the truth. Not only will your colleague appreciate the positive feedback, but you will settle your score with the universe. And the more positive energy you put out, the more positive energy you receive back. There's no harm or shame in being the person in the office that everyone feels like they can talk to. Those individuals have an incredible amount of influence and are often responsible for tying office members together as they build the bridge between aloof professionalism and authentic communication.

A good way to think of "completing" is to imagine it as a deep cleaning, as opposed to just clearing up the clutter. If you're really looking to clean your house or desk at your office, you'll have completed the job thoroughly if you commit yourself to cleaning *everything* rather than just shifting the clutter out of sight. Shifting the clutter, similar to not *completely* sharing your emotions, gets the job done passably in the meantime. But to really make a change and do what you've set out to accomplish, you need to go ahead with the deep cleaning and complete your emotions to your coworkers. Keeping your home and workspace clean keeps the day running smoothly, just like completing will do for your life.

SPEAKING UNARGUABLY

Part of the completing process is to speak unarguably throughout your day. You can do this by only saying what is true for you.

So many arguments could be amicably ended if people would only say what is true for them. Oftentimes, arguments go unresolved because people refuse to say what they really feel. They won't admit *why* they're hurting and where their anger is coming from. Or perhaps they are embarrassed about some of the things they're feeling, like jealousy or anger over something outside of their control. And although it may be difficult to really speak to the heart of the matter when in the middle of a tension-filled, emotional argument, it's truly the only way a conflict can get resolved.

> Do say what is true for you.

Don't get caught up in the "he said, she said" of an argument; just speak unarguably and you can cut the time of your arguments in half. So when you're in the midst of a heated argument, how do you speak unarguably?

Source a physical sensation

For instance, you could say, "I noticed that when you yell at me, my heart races." A statement like that is unarguable, as no one can tell what does or doesn't make your heart race or your stomach hurt. Also, it prevents the blame game from occurring by ensuring that it's not blatantly directed at the other person but, rather, translated into something that they could understand and relate to themselves. Oftentimes, people get defensive when they feel like they're being blamed for something they feel they didn't do. Instead, start from a common ground and source emotions and thoughts with which you both can identify.

Source an emotion

Your emotions are always the truth. No matter what the situation, no one can tell you that what you're feeling is not what you're feeling. Although emotions don't always derive from logic or a place of ease in understanding, they are still true and can be regarded in some way or another.

When you're sourcing an emotion, it's most effective to source one of the five key emotions so that the listener understands exactly what you are feeling. For example, "I felt sad when we lost that client." The five key emotions are a color wheel of sorts; they are the emotions that work together to combine other various emotions that we feel.

When sourcing an emotion it's important to remember that you can't throw that emotion in the other person's face and say that "because you're making me feel angry, obviously it's you who is in the wrong." Rather, source your emotions, explain why and when you feel that particular emotion, and work with the other individual to see why they create that particular emotion within you and how that can be avoided or helped in the future.

Repeat your thoughts to yourself first

This one can be tricky, because what we think of as facts often aren't. Every memory is biased in some way, because it comes from a single perspective while each situation can be evaluated and reviewed through multiple perspectives. So if your coworker is doing something that is bothering you and you want to approach them about it, first repeat what you want to say to yourself. If what you're saying is a judgment rather than a fact, then you know you need to rephrase it into something factual before approaching your coworker.

For example, is it really "true" that your coworker was rude to you and is therefore a rude person? Perhaps you thought so, but is that stating a fact? No. So what actually led you to this judgment? It *is* true that your coworker interrupted you in a meeting and that she has interrupted in the past three meetings as well. Start with the fact and then explain how it makes you feel. Your coworker can't argue with a fact and how it makes you feel, but they do have an argument if you have no facts to support what you're saying. Just remember, facts can't be disputed, but personal judgments can.

Don't hold things back

When you withhold the truth from your coworkers (such as how you feel when your project mate takes credit for your brainchild or your office mate blasts music from her speakers), your anger and sadness fester. Over time it becomes powerful and larger than life, even if the issue is a minor concern. If you let it fester to this point, then the issue becomes a vastly greater deal than it was initially, and it's more difficult to rectify.

This is why so many people tend to snap over seemingly innocuous things—the truth is they have been holding in their emotions for so long that when they finally let loose, their emotional output is far beyond what it needs to be.

The lesson? Never keep withholds from your colleagues or your clients. Although it may feel awkward or uncomfortable sharing your feelings in the moment, it will be a much greater issue if you explode two months down the line and they wonder why you never discussed the problem with them in the first place. Additionally, withholding how you feel or what you're thinking from a coworker, boss, or client is inauthentic and doesn't allow for a true relationship with any of these parties. How do you expect to achieve any sort of productivity if you're withholding how you really feel from the people with whom you're supposed to have the closest relationship? Answer: you can't, and your work will be greatly hindered by your lack of communication.

Do yourself and your work environment a favor by releasing your withholds and practicing up-front and honest communication. (Sexual feelings in the office are the exception to this rule. Process these alone.)

Remain unarguable

You can't create an environment of authentic communication if you don't have certain boundaries in place. Expressing your thoughts and feelings is key to authentic communication, but if you don't express them in a way that is useful or understandable to your colleagues, you are only going to complicate the communication in your office and in your life. The best way to make sure your communication is both authentic and useful is to remain unarguable. This means following the above steps (sourcing an emotion or physical sensation, or recalling a state of events) and sharing your feedback as it arises. Don't wait until the feelings become unmanageable and you snap. Positive change rarely comes out of such stressed communication.

Office Scene: An Attitude Shift

The Scene: Leeks, Inc., a legal consulting firm

The Problem: Turning complaints into requests

The People: Jim (a legal consultant), Janet (his assistant)

Generally, the employees at Leeks, Inc., are a very satisfied, motivated group of individuals. Across the board they all have strong work ethics, great relationships with their clients and each other, and they enjoy coming to work each day. The management staff works hard to ensure that they've created a positive work environment where their employees can thrive.

And for the most part they've been successful. Except for Jim.

Jim has been with Leeks for over ten years now, and when new employees discover this they often wonder why, as Jim seems to do nothing but complain, complain, complain. Every day he complains that the office is too cold, that lunch can't come soon enough, that his clients are the most difficult to work with, that he can't focus with all of the noise from his coworkers, that his bosses don't respect him and don't care about the hard work he puts in. It's never-ending! It's gotten so bad that all of his coworkers make it a point to stay far away from him, for he exudes such negative energy no one can stand to be around him. Because Jim hasn't realized that he is actually the cause of his coworkers' distance, it's only more fodder for complaint when he gripes about how there is no one in the office who understands him.

Because Jim has been with the firm for awhile and handles a lot of Leeks' big clients, he is given an assistant, Janet, to help him with paperwork, filing, and other organizational tasks. Although Janet is a kind, sweet, very hardworking young woman, Jim couldn't be more rude and aggressive when asking her to do certain tasks. And, of course, nothing is ever done the way he would have done it. His complaints range from "I can't believe you put this paperwork in *that* file—it doesn't go there!" to "I'd be able to stay a lot more organized if you were better at keeping my desk and office space clean" to "Why can't you move more quickly, Janet? How am I supposed to get everything done if you can't keep up with me?" and "I wish they had never given me an assistant. I could get all of my work done more efficiently if I were just doing it myself." The day that Jim throws this last complaint at Janet, she finally has had enough.

"Listen, Jim," she begins nervously, "I've been taking your complaints and criticisms for a long time now, and frankly, I'm sick of it. And I know that no one else is going to come forward to voice their opinions, but everyone else in this office is sick of you, too. We're sick of your negativity, we're sick of your bitter attitude, and we're sick of the fact that you can never request anything from anyone without turning it into a complaint. I don't know what happened that has made you so bitter and unhappy, but you're not doing yourself any favors by taking it out on your coworkers."

With that, Janet takes a deep breath, gathers her things, and says, "I deserve much better than what you put me through every day. I quit." And she walks out, leaving a shocked, gaping Jim in her tracks. At first he is fuming. *How dare she talk to me that way!* he thinks to himself, astonished at what has just happened. No one has ever stood up to him like that before! As he spends the rest of the afternoon alone in his office, he has a lot of time to think. Initially he is incredibly upset and feels that Janet has been way out of line. But then he realizes that after ten years of working for Leeks he is incredibly successful in his professional life but doesn't have any close personal relationships with his coworkers, or really any happiness at all. With that startling realization, he vows to turn his attitude around and to stop being such a bitter, unhappy, over-complaining individual.

He starts first with his coworkers, calling them all into the conference room to offer a formal apology. "Hey everyone," he starts, "Janet just alerted me to the fact that I've become quite a negative presence here in the office, and I just wanted to issue a formal apology to everyone for how I've been acting and for any hurt that my poor attitude may have caused. From this day forward, I vow to adjust my attitude and turn my complaints into requests rather than just barking unhappiness at you all every day. We're all on the same page here, and it's not fair for me to be imposing the negativity that I have been. I really hope you'll forgive me."

Although apologizing is a difficult thing for him to do, Jim notices the positive reaction from his coworkers immediately. They seem relieved that Jim has come forward to issue such an apology, and as the week goes on they encourage Jim's new attitude and remind him when some of his complaints could be rephrased as requests. On the whole, Leeks, Inc., is all the better because of it.

As for Janet, Jim calls her immediately after his meeting with his coworkers to issue her a formal apology. "Janet, I just wanted to call and say that I am terribly sorry for the way I was treating you. You have always been an excellent assistant, and I was wrong to take advantage of you and be so negative in how I treated you. I also owe you a huge thank-you for having the guts to stand up to me and tell me how you and everyone else were feeling. I'm going to be making a lot of changes in how I treat people and how I used to complain about things, and I'd really love it if you'd come back as my assistant again."

Janet can tell what she said really has resonated with Jim, and she is heartened by how immediately he has taken her words to heart. "Jim, I really appreciate your calling and being so receptive to what I was saying. I would love to come back as your assistant; I didn't really want to quit anyhow!"

Janet comes back the next day and is shocked by how much more pleasant Jim is to work with. Although he still has gripes, just like anyone in the office, he is conscious of turning them into requests rather than just complaining about everything all the time. Jim is much happier, and the whole of Leeks, Inc., is thrilled with their new relationship with Jim.

PULLING OUT YOUR SHOULD-ER

It is all too easy to slip into inauthentic communication. In fact, half of the time we don't even realize we are doing it! Some of the phrases that we commonly use, such as "should" or "need to," set us up for patterns of inauthentic communication. This is because such phrases come with emotional strings attached, strings that pull on both the listener and the speaker.

For example, when you use the word "should," you transmit the idea that someone or something is not how it is supposed to be or how it ought to be. When you get angry with your coworker for not pitching in on a project and you tell her, "You *should* be helping me more," what your *should* is really saying is, "You *should* be more respectful of me and my time."

What's so bad about that? Well, you can't tell anyone how to feel or think, nor do you have the ability to put your should-er out there and demand positive results.

All your should-er does is put the listener on the defensive ("Why should I have to do that?") and it also entrenches you further in your personas ("I am entitled to feel this way, because you should have treated me better!") Whoa—you can see how when shoulds start flying, any hope for resolution and authentic communication goes out the window.

The next time you find yourself using the word "should," whether it is out loud or in your head, try rooting the word out. Just by removing the word "should" (or similar phrases like "need to," "ought to," etc.) from your vocabulary and finding a less dramatic replacement for it, you can create a more authentic conversation and shift out of the persona. So the next time you find yourself telling someone what they should do or telling yourself how you should feel, put on the brakes!

> There is no room for "shoulds" in the universe or in the workplace—things are as they are, and you won't successfully "should" your way to a more positive work life.

You can, however, create a more positive office life by being authentic. For example, instead of "I should be making more money" or "I need to be making more money," say "I want to make more money." When you make your wants clear by stating them outright, you can better visualize what steps you need to take in order to make those dreams a reality. When you state that you need or should make more money, you end up feeling passed over and unappreciated, as if you're not working to your potential or not being fairly compensated. Rephrasing this to state that you "want" to make more money helps you to feel motivated and empowered; your goal is clear and you feel in charge of your destiny. You can then see ways you can make more money (such as by landing a new client or asking for a raise) instead of just sitting around and feeling sorry for yourself.

To that end, everything in the universe is as it should be, because the universe is always supporting you completely. It's important to find the reasons behind things instead of allowing pain and strife to be all-consuming and the be-all and end-all to your situation. For example, perhaps you had to stay late for work, but you wound up missing a car accident on the freeway that would have kept you in a traffic jam for the same period of time. Maybe a big account you wanted was given to another one of your coworkers, but that kept you open to be able to work on an even bigger account that was more your interest anyway.

> The way things work out always steers your life in the direction it needs to go, and using words like "should" or "need" thwarts that.

The words "should" and "need" frame circumstances as something negative rather than perfect, as all things are.

Ditch the "shoulds" and "needs" in your life and welcome authenticity in their place, and you will see the difference in your relationships and thought processes almost immediately.

SHIFTING COMPLAINTS

When you spend the majority of your day in an enclosed office space with your coworkers, there isn't anything worse than being in a room filled with disgruntled, unsatisfied individuals. Even if you walk into the office in an optimistic, fun-loving mood, your spirits can be shattered by the constant complaints and whining of those around you. Even worse, you might be part of the problem! If you find yourself stuck in a negative, toxic, and complaining mood, it might be time for a shift in communication.

A positive shift in communication can not only improve your mood, but it can also improve the mood of those around you and make you a more pleasant person to be around. Here's how to do it.

Turn your complaints into requests

A great device for averting negative communication is converting your complaints into requests. Complaints are the dark underbelly of requests—once you flip them right side up, the request is waiting there, waiting to become positive. Once you've turned a complaint upside down and found the request, you can move forward in a more positive, uplifting manner. You'll also realize quickly how easy it is to make something seemingly negative become a positive. Here are some examples of complaints that have been turned into requests:

Complaint: This office is so cold.

Request: Would anyone mind if I turned the heat up? I'm feeling a little chilly.

Complaint: I hate the coffee here.

Request: I'd like to freshen things up a bit and request a different brand of coffee. Anyone else agree?

Complaint: This client has a major attitude problem.

Request: This email tone is a little abrupt, and to be honest, I think it undermines me as a peer and as a person. Could you please talk to me more respectfully in the future?

Complaint: I hate my coworker; she is so lazy.

Request: I think that you aren't pulling your weight on this project, and it is making me frustrated. Can we discuss how this can be changed in the future?

As you can imagine, not every request is going to be met with a positive response. Maybe your fellow coworkers do like the coffee, or maybe your client doesn't think the tone of their email is harsh and could be offensive. Even so, by rephrasing your complaints and delivering them as requests, you increase your chances of receiving a positive response, and then you're not the one responsible for creating an angry, toxic work environment. It's true that you can't always have what you want, but it's better to request to change something that's making you unhappy in a way that isn't abrasive toward others than to whine and complain and expect those around you to listen and respond regardless.

Be honest with your requests

Sometimes turning complaints into requests is the easy part. Phrasing the request is what causes the difficulty. Instead of literally rephrasing their complaints, people often try to disguise their requests so that they don't come off as demanding, or so that people might think the request is more of a suggestion. Consider an employer who asks his employees, "Hey, do you think you guys want to come in on Saturday?" Of course, no one *wants* to come in on a Saturday! However, the employer thought that by phrasing his request this way, he could soften the blow and make it seem as though he wasn't a demanding employer. But what he really did was irritate and confuse his employees, leading them to wonder, "Does he really think any of us want to work on the weekends? Does he think this is a treat for us? Can I say no to this, or is it mandatory?"

A better way to have gone about this might have been to just email or gather the employees together and say, "Everyone, we need to work on Saturday to finish this deadline. It's not fun to work on the weekends, I know that. But it's what we need to do, so let's make the best of it." By rephrasing the request and also qualifying the fact that he knows they aren't going to be happy, and that it's not fun, he shows the employees that their feelings are being heard, that he understands how they feel, and that it is important to him. If you're honest with your requests but you phrase them in a way that truly considers the other person, then you're much more apt to get a positive response. When you complain, you bring negative energy into someone else's space without their asking for it. It's fine to be unhappy with something, but it's not fine to place that unhappiness on someone else and to expect them to still want to take care of it for you.

Request what you want, not what you don't want

When you request what you don't want ("Oh my God, I really hope we don't have to work late tonight") instead of what you do want ("Let's work really hard so that we can finish on time today"), it doesn't lead to a solution as clearly. By saying what you don't want to do (work late), you are basically just complaining without any clear solution. But notice how when you say what you do want (to finish on time), a solution (working hard) seems to come almost immediately to mind. By encouraging an end goal, you are sharing your request with your coworkers, who are more apt to respond to something shared and communal than something negative and singular. Generally, what you don't want to do is probably what someone else doesn't want to do, so what good does it do for you to complain about it?

This is especially true when it comes to management issues. When you tell your employees what you don't want—tardiness—all they hear is an imagined insult. "Is he saying that I'm late?" they wonder. "I haven't been late once in the past six months; why is he all of a sudden telling us to not be late?" Also, the manager in this situation hasn't effectively addressed the issue. If the problem is that the rule isn't being followed, then it does no good to go to each of your employees to simply restate that rule.

Instead try phrasing your requests by telling employees what you do want or what the problem actually is. For example, "It is our intention to have you work an eight-hour day and not more. I have noticed that some of you do not start your workday at 9:00 a.m. If you are unable to do so, please talk to me and we can arrange different hours for you. Otherwise, please be working by 9:00 a.m. in accordance with company policy." This tactic proves to be much more effective in that it directly addresses the issue and calls for a solution to the problem rather than not dealing with the problem or coming up with a way to solve it.

Or, for example, if you have an employee who talks too much during meetings, don't tell her what you don't want ("Can you please not talk so much during meetings?"). Instead tell her what you do want ("I want you to be more strategic about what you say during meetings."). This way your intentions are clearer and your employee better understands what her plan of action should be. Also, she will be less likely to be offended by a request that is phrased positively, which will keep her mood from dampening and keep her proactive about the changes she needs to make.

In any typical office, when you're sitting at the same desk with the same people all day, there will undoubtedly be things that irk you and make you angry or frustrated. That's entirely okay. It's abusing your coworkers with your frustration that isn't. So next time you want to voice a complaint, remember to rephrase it as a request. Both you and your coworkers will be much, much happier.

REAP THE BENEFITS

When you speak unarguably, you make it easier for your listener to accept your feedback. Since you are framing your stories in an obviously subjective way (such as "I feel that..." or "I have a story that..."), you make it easier for your colleague to digest what you are saying without taking offense. When you speak unarguably, you can speak to everyone from your boss to a five-year-old in a successful and authentic manner. This means you decrease the feelings you hurt and increase the positive changes in your life.

- When you speak unarguably, you remove inauthentic communication from your life. You "clean up" your communication and keep it honest and to the point.

- It is impossible to speak from an unbiased perspective, and it is also impossible to speak from an unemotional standpoint. That's okay. As long as you admit that your statements are influenced by your emotions and that you might be making up stories, you can keep your subjective viewpoint from hampering communication.

CHAPTER 8

TURN OFF THE NOISE

HOW TO CREATE WORK/LIFE BALANCE

The time you enjoy wasting is not wasted time.

—Bertrand Russell

Productivity, and the way to achieve it, is misunderstood in most American companies. A mistake many employers make is that they believe the more hours they squeeze out of employees, the more the company can produce, sell, or service. My personal belief is that well-rested employees with finite schedules feel more happiness and become more productive. Joyfulness and productivity go hand in hand. Anyone who says, "It's work, so you can't enjoy it" is going to find that they have a lot of employee turnover.

> Having a sense of fairness about how you are treated and how and when you work is a source of great aliveness for employees and allows them to be present and focused.

Dread, exhaustion, anger, and depression do not serve a company well. These are the fruits of an overbearing schedule, one in which the employee's feeling of control over her or his life is removed. Instead of rating employees based on how many hours they are clocked in, or how often they let their vacation days go to waste, employees can be rated based on the work they produce, including both quality and quantity.

Of course, this doesn't mean that employees are permitted to be lazy and unproductive. At Empower PR we expect all of our employees to put in an eight-hour workday—but not more. We religiously give employees the weekend off, because as a PR firm, we have clients on weekend segments all of the time. If our employees went to all of these segments, they would never have a day off to rest. For this reason, we make "no work on the weekends" part of our policy.

Here is how you can begin creating this work/life balance in your own life:

Office Scene: When Work Takes Over
The Scene: Gage Recruiting Firm
The Problem: Lack of work/life balance

The People: Lindsay (a recruiter), Jack (her boss), Rob (her husband)

Lindsay has been a recruiter with Gage Recruiting for about three years and is very happy with her job. She has recently been promoted to senior recruiter and has been given increased responsibility and more challenging assignments. She likes her coworkers and goes out for the occasional happy hour with them on Friday evenings. She likes her boss, Jack, too. He seems to genuinely appreciate her hard work and is very fair with everyone. In previous jobs Lindsay felt she may have been overlooked for promotions or raises because other employees had more of a personal friendship with the boss, but Jack doesn't play favorites.

One Friday night Jack approaches Lindsay and asks her if she would be able to come in the next day to finish up a project a bit early. Lindsay, feeling excited that her boss is entrusting this responsibility to her, is more than happy to oblige. But what is originally a one-time request begins becoming a routine. Suddenly Jack is asking Lindsay to stay late and come into the office on weekends more and more often. Even when she isn't at work, Jack is texting her or emailing her on her BlackBerry with work-related questions and problems, often in the late evening. It is starting to take a toll on her marriage and her sanity.

One night Lindsay is out to dinner with her husband,

Rob. Rob has planned a romantic dinner at one of their favorite restaurants so they can have some quality alone time together. It seems that lately they are always busy with work or social engagements, and they never really get a moment to be alone with each other. Just after the waiter has poured them each a glass of wine, Lindsay's BlackBerry vibrates.

"I don't understand why you bring that thing with you everywhere," huffs Rob, as the annoying device ruins yet another evening. "It's 7:00 p.m. on a Friday night; you're not on call, you know."

"I know. I'm just not sure how to approach him about this," says Lindsay, as she looks down to read the newest email Jack has sent. "I don't want to get passed over for another promotion because my boss doesn't remember that I exist. I guess I should take it as a compliment that he is always thinking of me when things need to get done, but I feel like my entire life revolves around work." Lindsay excuses herself from the table to respond to her boss's email.

Lindsay and Rob discuss the problem the entire ride home, and Lindsay feels confident enough the next morning to approach her boss about the situation.

"I feel as though I'm always on call, and it's starting to affect my personal life, including my relationship with my husband," explains Lindsay to Jack. "As happy as I am that you are always contacting me for work-related projects, I'm beginning to worry that my job performance will start to deteriorate if I don't have an adequate personal life to balance it."

"I had no idea, Lindsay," says Jack, alarmed at how much her job is getting to her. "I never want my employees to become afraid of their BlackBerrys or to feel the need to take it with them wherever they go. I think that by coming forward you have actually helped the entire company with its work/life balance."

That day, Jack decides to institute a new policy at the office—no more using BlackBerrys after hours. He tells all of his employees that they are no longer required to answer calls or emails after 6:00 p.m. on the weekdays or at all on the weekends.

Since the policy has been put in place, everyone at Gage Recruiting is a lot happier, including Lindsay. Jack has noticed the change, too. His employees are no longer hesitant to take on a new project now that they don't have to worry about having to come in on Saturday to finish it up. They also have more energy and actually accomplish more during the workday, since they're not tired from working late the night before. Jack is very happy that he realized that work/life balance is essential to happy employees and a productive workplace.

EMPLOYEE APPRECIATION

A big part of creating a work/life balance is appreciation.

> When you are appreciated, you feel comforted and rejuvenated, and you take a moment to reflect, rest, and feel proud of your accomplishments.

Appreciations are psychically refreshing and curative. An atmosphere of crunches, deadlines, and little appreciation leads to incredible work stress that can be hard to let go.

Treating employees like adults and letting them set up their hours (and make up missed hours if need be, such as for doctor's visits and the like) is worth its weight in gold when it comes to employee productivity and morale. This doesn't mean allowing employees to set up their hours willy-nilly. In fact, I have found the opposite result to take place. Due to the feeling of community and friendship within the office, everyone has a sense of responsibility and a desire to pull their own weight—no one wants to stick their friend with extra work or leave their friend high and dry for a television segment.

Several organizations have become famous for allowing employees to work from home or not requiring all of their work hours to be spent in the office, but it is my belief that the "work from home" model makes it difficult for frequent collaboration. Instead it is more effective to work in an environment where rest and autonomy are part of the work-day and allow employees to be responsible for how their time in the office is spent.

NO-EMAIL TIMES

Allowing employees to carry work home with them and never take mental breaks is a huge management mistake that many companies make. For this reason, my employees and I stick to a no-email policy after 6:00 p.m. or before 6:00 a.m., and no emails *period* on the weekends. Some employees still check their BlackBerrys regularly anyway in case there is a press request, a deadline, or a time-sensitive client matter, but in general, our work community rests. PDAs and email can be very addictive, and stopping the noise as a group keeps these addictions from taking root.

When the world found out about our no-email policy, the famous business TV program *Your World with Neil Cavuto* had me on the program, and the Sunday *New York Times* business section covered the story. After realizing how un-usual and tantalizing this policy was to the rest of the world, it became clear to me that our policy was necessary and beneficial. Indeed, there are times when I check my email every sixty seconds—so stopping the madness at night and on the weekends is the only way to rest and rejuvenate for the coming workday.

BREAKS IN THE OFFICE

Work/life balance also must include regular breaks. The theory of "work, rest, recover" is used by everyone from Olympic athletes to NASA scientists as a preferred method of employment. Just as athletes need to rest their bodies between workout days in order to allow muscles to heal and grow, employees need to rest their minds during the workday in order to promote creativity and clear thinking. Without sufficient rest, an employee's work will certainly suffer.

This is why all of my staff begins their workday by reading the paper and drinking coffee together in the break room. So often employees dread going into work, turning on the computer, and beginning the rat race. This dread dissipates if employees can come in to work, have some coffee, and talk among each other, sparking both creativity and fun, and bouncing ideas for the weekly pitches off of one another. Not only is reading the news and being informed a big part of being a successful publicist, but it also allows employees to bond, relax, and recharge before a grueling day of work.

My employees are also given a one-hour lunch break at noon, and lunch is provided at no cost. This includes soda, coffee, snacks, and frozen meals, all of which are in addition to the lunch we order in every day. By providing your team with healthy, delicious food, you can turn lunch into a productive part of your company's day. Instead of a group of lethargic employees in a food coma due to McDonald's, you could have active, creative employees who feel healthy and invigorated after lunch. Not only does this save my employees money and time—since they don't have to run out to buy their lunch or coffee—but it also gives everyone a chance to enjoy lunch together. We all gather at noon and share lunch, which keeps my team cohesive and friendly. From president to intern, lunch is a time when we can all join together as a team of equals, and the conversation and laughter creates a happy environment that lasts well into the afternoon.

This environment of friendliness and fun extends throughout the workday. From coffee breaks to casual conversations in the hallway and in the offices, employees are encouraged to socialize and congregate as they deem appropriate. Instead of treating employees like automatons and their desks as cages, we allow employees to use their daytime work hours as they see fit—if they spend too much time talking and don't get their work done, they will be the ones who have to stay late to finish their projects. Thus, in the end, even though talking is allowed, most people keep their socializing to a minimum so they can leave work on time every night.

Another way I have found to achieve work/life balance is to create "summer hours" for my employees. During the summer hours, employees can leave at 3:00 p.m. on Fridays and come back to the office at 10:30 a.m. on Mondays. This creates a feeling of a "long weekend" that negates the need for employees to take a week off for vacation in the summertime. And since my employees know they have a little time off, they work extra hard during the week so that they can take advantage of the summer hours and enjoy their time off.

CLIENT/EMPLOYEE RELATIONS

Another important component of work/life balance is how employers and clients treat employees when on the job. If you are expected to take it on the chin from an angry client or an angry boss, the rest of your work life almost doesn't matter. If you are not treated respectfully, joyfulness will not prevail and productivity will be low. This is why I insist that all employees at Empower PR be treated courteously and kindly by their clients, and vice versa.

This bargain is struck at the beginning of every relationship that we form with our clients. We explain that we want to be treated like peers and spoken to with respect, and in return we will deliver the same style of communication, along with our hard work on their account. If a client veers from this respectful communication during our relationship, a change in behavior is requested. If the requested behavior doesn't happen, we fire the client. And, of course, it goes without saying that an employee who is rude or disrespectful would receive the same treatment. No one has to suffer through poor treatment to work at Empower PR—suffering isn't part of the job requirement.

SOCIAL OUTINGS

Another component of work/life balance involves creating social situations for employees to connect. Beyond the typical corporate holiday party, outings for achieving revenue benchmarks and group dinners with everyone's significant others at the boss's house are part of the social events at Empower PR. Employees don't usually want to play with the boss, but they want to know that they can, and they want to be known and understood as the person they are, not as just another cog in the corporate wheel.

Thus, there are many keys to creating a successful work/life balance. And some of them are a little easier than others to institute in the workplace. The equation is simple: ensure that your employees are able to maintain their personal connections; have clear schedules and days when they can focus on their own lives; and receive fair treatment from each other, management, and clients. These three things are integral to creating a successful work/life balance, and having a successful work/life balance is the key to having a healthy lifestyle.

LIVE FOR YOUR ALIVENESS

Many people have goals that they think will make them happy if they can just achieve them, such as owning a nice car, having a big family, making a lot of money, or being the boss. Whatever your goals are, your primary focus can be on one thing—living for your own aliveness. What does this mean?

When you live for your aliveness (also known as living in the present, being in ease and flow, being in essence), you are engaged, present, and have almost a prickly sense of enthusiasm and a bubbly spirit. The world is not something you are observing or something you are worrying about—it is something that you are a part of, and that is a part of you. You can tell when someone you meet is living for their aliveness. Their eyes are clear and bright, their mood is open, their viewpoint is positive, and usually they are also quite successful in their career of choice. This is because someone who lives for their aliveness chooses a career about which they are passionate and enthusiastic.

By choosing a career based on personal fulfillment (instead of how much money it pays or how lucrative the venture might turn out to be) you are guaranteed to be happier and more in love with your day-to-day life. You won't dread going into work or working hard. What you do at work becomes just another extension of your happy, positive life.

I am living proof of this. After being in business as a venture capitalist for most of my life, I had made a lot of money and become very successful in my field. But I wasn't happy. I didn't get a thrill of excitement or pleasure about the work I was doing. Then one day I noticed that I *did* feel this excitement when I was helping my wife, leading sex thera-pist Dr. Laura Berman, prep with the producers for her many television appearances. I enjoyed the creative aspect of com-ing up with new, fresh topics and talking points, and I liked the idea that her words were reaching and helping millions of people across the world.

That's when I knew that public relations was the field for me. I left the venture capitalist world and never looked back. Gone were the days of fundraising, schmoozing, and frantic budget meetings. Gone were the days when all I thought about was how to save money and cut corners. Now I could do what I truly loved—be creative and be part of the media world.

Years later this dream of mine has become a flourishing reality. I went from leading my wife's public relations ef-forts to having thirty clients in all different fields, including lifestyle, hospitality, health and wellness, and restaurants. Not only do I love what I do, I love what my clients do, and I love going into one of my client's restaurants and enjoying the fried green tomatoes dish that I just landed on WGN. I have created the perfect life for myself—all my living is for my aliveness and doing what feels good instead of what is allegedly lucrative. By doing what I love, letting go of control, and believing the universe will sup-port me, I learned to be in majesty and have a career that I love.

- When you don't have a work/life balance and you spend all of your time working, you negatively affect your mood, your health, your creativity, and your peace of mind.

- By taking regular breaks to recharge your batteries and relax, you are actually doing a service to your employers and your clients, because they need you to be running on all four cylinders.

- Use your vacation days, sleep in late every once in awhile, and take a moment to enjoy a cup of coffee with your colleagues. Your work will improve as a result.

CHAPTER 9

OWN YOUR 100%

BRINGING RESPONSIBILITY
BACK TO THE OFFICE

Let everyone sweep in front of his own door, and the whole world will be clean.

—Johann Wolfgang von Goethe

When you enter a No-Gossip Zone, you begin to take responsibility for the words you say and for your communication style. However, taking full responsibility for your actions requires more than just ceasing to gossip.

Office Scene: Owning Your 100%

The Scene: Revolution, Inc., a real estate firm

The Problem: Not owning your 100%

The People: Kevin (a real estate broker), Rich (his boss)

Kevin is a real estate broker in Macon, West Virginia. For two years he has worked for Revolution, Inc., but has yet to land a raise or a promotion, despite landing some great deals early in his time there. Angry about being passed over for these rewards, Kevin routinely slacks off when on the job. He calls in sick a few times a month, and he always comes in late and leaves early. During his time at work, Kevin checks his fantasy football stats, snacks in the break room, and otherwise goofs off.

Everyone at Revolution, Inc., likes Kevin, but his coworkers often dread his presence at lunch and happy hour, because he often kills everyone else's good mood by complaining about work and tooting his own horn. Even though Kevin is a happy-go-lucky person for the most part, his demeanor at work is often surly and grumpy, mainly because he feels ignored and underappreciated. He is especially bitter that he recently asked for a raise and was turned down by his boss, Rich, with the explanation that he needs to work harder in order to deserve a raise.

However, instead of working harder, Kevin has started working even less. Finally, Rich decides he has no other recourse but to give Kevin a warning. He sits Kevin down in his office for a heart-to-heart about the possible outcomes if Kevin continues slacking off: "Kevin, you have been with us for a long time. We like you here. But lately your work has been sloppy and unfocused. The way your work currently is—well, if it keeps up, or God forbid, gets worse, I am going to have to let you go."

Kevin is shocked. "What do you mean?" he splutters. "Let *me* go? I have been a loyal and hardworking employee for over two years!"

"That's not exactly true," corrects Rich. "Yes, you have been here two years, but your work has really tapered off recently. It's like you don't want to be here."

"I knew no one here appreciated me! Don't you realize that I have helped to make this company what it is? What about the Markson account? And the Jacobs house? Who do you think nabbed us those accounts? I outsold every other broker here in those months!"

"That was a year and half ago, Kevin! What have you done recently? I can't reward you for something that happened months ago!"

"Well, you didn't reward me at the time either, did you? I haven't gotten a single raise or promotion since I started here! I am the only employee here who hasn't!" Kevin points out.

"I know that. But that's because you did great work a couple of times and then gave up. If you want a raise or a promotion at Revolution, you have to prove that you do good work consistently. Face it—you didn't get a raise immediately after the Markson and Jacobs wins, so you gave up! Do you realize you have been basically pouting ever since then? You haven't worked hard on an account since," declares Rich angrily.

Kevin opens his mouth to argue, but he can't think of a defense. For the first time, he realizes his part in creating the situation he resents. He realizes that he needs to own his 100% of his lack of career success. He hesitates before speaking but then says, "Some of what you say— okay, all of what you say is true. I have screwed up. I have had a bad attitude. I know that. I could tell by the way people looked at me here that I wasn't in the right."

Rich sighs. "Listen, let's just start over. I was wrong in not commending you enough for the Jacobs job, and I didn't speak to you about your attitude soon enough. But we hired you for a reason and we want you here. Let's just be more open and honest with each other from now on. If you need my appreciation, tell me. I am not always the sharpest tool in the shed."

Kevin laughs, "It's a deal."

OWNING YOUR 100%

When we experience happiness, we don't feel the need to automatically shove that onto someone else, do we? No, because it makes us feel good, so we prefer to own that emotion and its effects. The same holds true for negative feelings. If you can own your happiness, you can own your sadness, and soon you'll find that everything in your world is entirely within your control.

The key to tapping into your own internal power is to own your 100% of every situation you find yourself in and by owning every emotion you feel and thought you have. That means taking responsibility for yourself, instead of placing the blame and fault at the hands of someone else.

When you give other people the power to make you feel or think a certain way, you are subconsciously putting yourself under their control. Rather than taking complete responsibility for how you react to a situation, you are relinquishing your power and giving the reins to someone else. The unfortunate reality is that some of us give strangers on the street more ability to dictate our moods and frame of mind than we give ourselves. Although it's a perfectly normal reaction, once you start to turn that frame of mind around, you'll see how damaging it has been. It's an incredible waste of energy to give full power to someone who only impacts a fleeting moment of your day when you have to spend the rest of your day dealing with that.

It's true that a coworker or a certain situation may upset or anger you, but how you choose to react is entirely within your control. Taking responsibility for the way you feel and react to every situation you encounter can seem quite overwhelming. However, once you get the hang of the concept, you'll find that the exact opposite is true.

> As soon as you own your 100%, you are instantly empowered.

Once you begin to reclaim responsibility in your mind, you will regain your power and be able to effect positive changes in your current situation. You'll be able to own what you need to and let go of what you cannot impact. It doesn't mean that all negativity will recede, but you will learn to be at peace with those things that are unchangeable and to work to affect those things that are in your control.

HOW TO OWN YOUR 100%

> The first step to owning your 100% is to discover your role in the problems in the office.

A key element to discovering your role in your office's problems is being able to accept your own mistakes. It's easy to blame your higher-ups, your coworkers, and your clients for the current problems in the office, but that can't be the way you operate. In the entire scheme of things, it's unreasonable to expect that you can be without blame.

No one is perfect, and reassessing the way you process such things is a process all its own. Perhaps you didn't take the initiative on an important project. Maybe you dropped the ball in a new business meeting. It could be that when it comes to assessing a coworker's performance, you're too quick to judge. By taking responsibility for your mistakes, you can own your 100% and make your situation the best it can possibly be.

> The second step on the journey to owning your 100% is *to let go* of the festering grudges and petty jealousies that you have been keeping in the office.

You know that one guy who got the promotion over you last year (even though he totally didn't deserve it)? Let it go. The colleague who always blasts her music and wears ungodly smelling perfume? Move past it. Once you begin realizing that you and only you have the ability to accept these annoyances around you, they will cease to be bothersome.

There are only so many things of which you can take ownership. And when you are working to accomplish your own goals and responsibilities while at work, it's counterproductive to focus on what other people are doing, especially if the events occupying your mind are of an unnecessary nature and prevent you from completing your own tasks. If you can learn to let minor annoyances go, they will be mere background noise that you can tune out at will.

You can start accepting the annoying factors in your workplace by seeing them as part of a complete, perfect whole.

That is to say, your workplace is part of the universe's divine plan for you—right down to the perfume smell you hate, or the broken elevator. If you fight against these situations, you fight against your own reality and your own existence. It might also help to keep in mind that your own imperfections are no doubt annoying at times to people around you as well, so remember to offer them the same patience and respect you require from them.

DON'T OWN MORE THAN YOUR 100%

While it is important to own your 100% of every situation and not pass the buck, there is such a thing as owning too much. Often managers fall into this trap by trying to own 200, 300, or even 400% of their office's problems! Whenever something goes wrong in the office, they assume all the blame and shoulder all of the responsibility for fixing the error, even if they had nothing to do with the situation. Not only does this make for a stressed, unhappy manager, but it also means employees never learn to take on their 100%.

> When a manager, or an overeager employee, begins to own more than their own 100%, they become someone who needs to be in control all the time.

No one likes to work alongside a control freak, and certainly no one seeks to be managed by one.

If you're a manager, part of having a team is to know how to delegate. It's impossible for one person to run an entire company by themselves, and if you have a team of dedicated employees, why try? To ensure that you do not own more than your 100%, make sure that when you delegate responsibilities to your employees, you are actually delegating them. You're there for oversight and guidance if they need assistance, but you are not there to be looking over everyone's shoulder, making sure they are completing the tasks you've given them. If you know you are guilty of this type of "delegation," then you know that you own more than your share of the workload and that you aren't giving proper trust to your employees.

IT'S IN YOUR CONTROL

If everyone owned their 100% of every situation all the time, then everything would run much more efficiently. Employees would be concerned with accomplishing their tasks and contributing to the team instead of what everyone else is doing. In a strong, efficient work environment that is how colleagues function with one another. At the end of the day, you're the one living your life. What's the point in giving someone else all the control?

- Take responsibility for every situation in your life. You might not have caused all of them, but you have some role in allowing them to continue, even if it's only in your mind.
- Accept the negatives in your office, whether it is a small annoyance or a dislike for a coworker. You can't have perfection in your life, and when you accept this as part of the universe's divine plan, you can move past it.
- Don't take the blame for other people's mistakes. You are only responsible for yourself and your own actions.

CHAPTER 10

YOUR LOUDEST DENIALS ARE TRUE

AND OTHER PRINCIPLES

"Do unto others as you would have them do unto you."
—(Luke 6:31, NIV)

This section of the book includes other principles and nuggets of information regarding communication and the No-Gossip Zone that I believe are necessary to create the most authentic communication possible, as well as to manage your emotions and work environment effectively. Whether you're sourcing your emotions or completing them with your coworkers, these are helpful tips to keep in the back of your mind at all times.

YOU SPOT IT, YOU GOT IT

Judgmental thinking is always the result of something negative that you're feeling within yourself. You're jealous of a coworker who keeps landing big accounts, and the CEO loves every pitch she writes. And you say snidely to your coworkers, "Everyone just loves her because she's constantly sucking up to the boss. She's not really *that* talented."

Could it be, perhaps, that you're jealous because you're also overcompensating and putting in an exacerbated effort, yet you're just not achieving the same results? Once you pinpoint the root of those negative feelings, you realize that you're actually quite like that coworker who drives you so crazy. You're just upset because you aren't feeling as good about what you're doing.

It's the concept of "you spot it, you got it."

> We spot and dislike things in other people that we actually possess ourselves.

But when you spot it in someone else, it's a lot easier to point out what an awful person they are rather than admitting that you, too, possess those very same qualities. It's an easy trap to slip into, as judgment is a common tool that people use to make themselves feel better.

The trick to not letting those negative judgments overcome you is recognizing when you spot, or judge, something in someone else that is actually reminiscent of something you don't like about yourself. Not only does going through this mental process encourage you to become more authentic with yourself about the things within you that make you unhappy, but it also saves you from unfairly judging and developing resentment toward a coworker or friend who actually doesn't deserve it.

Office Scene: Looking Inward

The Scene: Fashion Pub, Inc.

The Problem: You spotted it!

The People: Lisa (a publicist), Rosie (a publicist)

Lisa and Rosie are both publicizing the same clothing retailer account. Lisa thinks of herself as someone with a strong, unwavering work ethic, excellent organizational skills, and a smart, logical head on her shoulders. When she sets out to do something, she doesn't rest until it has been successfully accomplished. Although she enjoys working with Rosie and considers her to be equally talented and motivated, she's become increasingly frustrated by how Rosie seems to micromanage everything she does. From calling her constantly to make sure she finishes projects, to asking for email updates all throughout the workday, Lisa is starting to feel as if she's being babysat rather than working collaboratively with a partner.

It's coming to the end of a very big media push for their client, and Rosie is growing increasingly stressed about getting everything done. To that end, Lisa's been feeling that Rosie is more controlling than ever. Finally, Lisa has had enough. One night while they are working late in the office, Lisa gets up the courage to confront Rosie about her trust issues. When Lisa brings up that she feels micromanaged by Rosie and hurt by her lack of trust in her ability to complete the projects and assignments she's committed to, Rosie seems a little surprised. "Lisa," she starts, "I'm terribly sorry if I've offended you in any way, but to be honest, when we began working together on this account, that's kind of how you were treating me. It seemed like you wanted to be the one in control, and I was getting a little frustrated, so perhaps I went too far in the other direction in order to assert myself in this partnership."

After Rosie has finished her explanation, Lisa thinks about what she has just heard before she responds to Rosie. Lisa has always known that she is a control freak, but after she thinks about the give-and-take of their partnership from beginning to end, she realizes that Rosie is exactly right. Lisa does have a bad habit of micromanaging and trying to overcontrol those she works with. "I'm sorry, Rosie. You're completely right. I know that I'm a control freak, but I guess it is so second nature to me, I didn't even realize that I was so aggressively overseeing everything you were doing. That's probably why your asserting your control bothered me so much, because I wanted to be the one in control rather than watching someone else take control of a situation. A partnership should be just that, a partnership, and I let my need to be a control freak get in the way of that."

"Oh, Lisa, don't worry about anything," Rosie says, kindly, "I do really enjoy working with you, and I think we make a great team. I'm sorry if pushed your buttons; I really wasn't trying to. But I really appreciate your taking my response to heart."

"Well," Lisa replies, "you certainly helped me learn my lesson, and I really appreciate that. From now on I'll try to check my need for control at the door."

WORK TOWARD WHAT YOU WANT, NOT WHAT YOU DON'T WANT

The philosophy of "manifesting" is quite the rage these days. Manifesting, or the idea that you can create positive events just by thinking about them, gets a lot of flak because people think it means that hard work isn't needed. However, that's not what manifesting is all about. Manifesting is just another word for positive thinking, and that is something every office needs if it is to be successful.

> One of the key components of achieving success is to believe you are capable of it.

This doesn't mean that just because you believe you're going to have the most reputable advertising agency in the country it will happen automatically, but it is a necessary part of pushing you toward that goal. When you think positively and set goals for what you do want (rather than obsessing about what you *don't* want or all of the things that could go wrong), you are more likely to succeed in your endeavors.

Think of it this way: how often do you work to accomplish something you don't really believe is possible? Probably not very often, because that wouldn't make much sense. If you approach your responsibilities with the frame of mind of "I can achieve this; this is possible," you will be that much more motivated to accomplish the goals before you. And your state of mind while working toward these goals will be much more peaceful and hence creative. When you let go of the "what ifs" and start imagining all the positive possibilities, you and your career will receive a boost.

> No one ever *what-if'd* themselves to success.

The manifestation of your goals needs to be rooted in a positive, forward-moving "I can" mentality.

One good way to start making positive thinking a regular part of your routine is to work toward goals that you are excited about and that make you happy. Manifesting requires an excitement for what you're doing. Although workdays have their boring, sluggish moments, it's important to always have a manifestation going for what you'd like to accomplish. Although everyone gets in ruts, how much easier would it be to keep your sights moving forward if you always had a positive manifestation that you were working toward? It's like a never-ending light at the end of the tunnel that keeps you motivated and positive.

For instance, if you work in a service industry and want to land your favorite sports team, you will be more likely to come across as passionate and involved than if you devote your sales efforts to a client you don't really enjoy. When you try to land clients you love and already feel passionately about, that positive energy and excitement will come across to the client as optimism and enthusiasm. This is all part of working toward what you want and making a commitment of joy and aliveness to yourself.

> The saying "Don't work harder, work smarter" might more accurately be phrased "Don't work harder, work happier."

When your work is joyous and full of meaning, everything you touch will manifest that positive energy and aliveness. When you trust that the universe is full of possibilities, you will never settle for anything less than brilliance, and your work will show results that you never before thought possible.

Managers must create systems that help employees discover their full potential rather than systems that allow employees to take no responsibility and hence no initiative. So the next time you find yourself taking on more blame than truly necessary, stop yourself. Don't play the hero to your staff or coworkers. To do so is actually insulting to their intelligence and abilities. Instead, ask them to own up to their mistakes, and then practice what you preach. Remember, don't manage *against* mistakes, manage *for* potential. The amount of mental energy you put in will be the same, but the output will be vastly different.

BUILDING CONFIDENCE

Instead of letting your insecurities hold you back, think about the worst thing that could happen if things go wrong. For example, you ask your boss for the promotion and he says no. But isn't knowing definitely that he said no better than wondering forever if he would have said yes? Isn't trying a new career better than living your life wondering if you would have been happier doing something different? None of these things are worse than letting a confidence issue get the better of you. And quite frankly, individuals who let a lack of self-confidence become the ruling force in their lives are stuck and not being authentic with themselves.

However, confidence requires building. It doesn't just exist on its own, and no one can make those things happen for you.

Don't let a lack of confidence manage your life. Take back the control and make things happen for yourself.

Office Scene: Eliminating Shyness

The Scene: Duhill, an ad agency

The Problem: Shyness gets in the way of success

The People: Jessica (an advertising executive), Jake (the CEO)

Jessica is an employee for a high-powered urban advertising agency, Duhill. She really enjoys her job and advertising is definitely one of her passions, but despite these things, she remains thwarted by the fact that she's constantly second-guessing herself. She has a hard time working in groups to come up with new advertising ideas, because she's afraid that if she speaks up and voices an opinion, her coworkers won't like it. But the ideas that she comes up with on her own are always very well received. Her concepts are very successful when they hit the market, and clients really appreciate her fresh and unique ideas.

Jessica knows she has issues with speaking up and that she tends to keep to herself, but her output is solid and she makes sure to get all of her work done on time, if not early. Because of this she's been a little confused as to why her coworkers have been getting promoted or given some of the more high-profile assignments when her work is just as good. But she is worried that if she speaks up and goes to her boss, he'll think she is being too aggressive or just complaining about her job. So she stays quiet and tries to really shine on the work that she is getting.

One afternoon her boss, Jake, surprises her in her office while she is putting together some materials for a new client. He asks to see what she is putting together, and Jessica is a little nervous, seeing as Jake isn't really known for visiting the offices of his employees. After he peruses her materials, he asks, "Jessica, are you happy here?"

She is very surprised. That certainly isn't what she was expecting when Jake came into her office. "Of course I am, Jake," she responds. "Why do you ask?"

"Well," he starts, "I'm always very impressed with the work you do, but you never seem very motivated to get it done. You never say a word during office meetings, you communicate mostly through email, and I never feel as if you're genuinely excited to be working on the accounts you're given."

Jessica doesn't even know what to say. She loves her job! She loves her accounts, the work she does, and she can't believe she is communicating the exact opposite. She says all of this to Jake and then explains that she is generally quiet because she thinks people don't really like her, or that maybe they are put off by some of her ideas.

"Jessica, you haven't ever given anyone a chance to know you. And although I think you have more ideas in your head than you actually share, I've always loved every concept you've come up with. I think you're incredibly talented and would have given you more work a long time ago if I had felt that you were as happy with your work as I am."

"I'm really sorry if I gave you the wrong impression, Jake. I hate to think that you've thought I'm not happy here. It's actually completely the opposite. I know I have insecure tendencies, and rather than working to overcome them I think I've let them get the better of me. I feel terrible that people have mistaken my insecurity as a lack of enthusiasm for my job, and I'm going to work hard to make sure my job performance is not hindered by my confidence issues."

"Well, Jessica," Jake responds, "I'm very, very glad to hear that. I think you have a lot of talent and the potential to really move forward here, both within our company and the industry itself. I'd hate to see your career held back because of insecurity."

"Thanks, Jake, that really means a lot to me. I promise you're going to see some definite changes in me."

After their meeting, Jessica makes a concerted effort to speak up, contribute, and share ideas with her coworkers. Once she is able to overcome her shyness and insecurity, she realizes that she works with some really terrific individuals and that she has a lot to bring to the company. After Jessica moves up the ladder within her company and gains some real professional credentials, she eventually starts her own advertising agency, never again to be thwarted by her own insecurities.

OUR LOUDEST DENIALS ARE ACTUALLY TRUE

Many times when something is true about us and we're not ready to admit it, we deny, deny, deny. It might be a good idea to reevaluate why it's important for you to so consistently deny that a certain event, or situation, or misgiving exists.

> Things that speak loudly to us generally have a deeper meaning, whether we're ready to admit that or not.

If it's recurring and it's impacting your life, then it's probably a good idea to reevaluate why it's developed such prominence in your day-to-day life. There is truth in your denials. To test for the truth in your denials, ask yourself these three questions:

- Is the denial is true?
- Are you completely sure that the denial is true? (Be open to any and all possible contradictions—even the most minute.)

- Is it possible that the opposite is true?

If you answer all three of these questions in affirmation, then you should consider whether or not the opposite might really be true. Any time you firmly resist accepting or understanding another person's viewpoint, you can be sure that a persona is at the helm, distorting your authentic communication.

Every individual employs a series of defense mechanisms to help them deal with things that are uncomfortable or difficult to handle. Denial is an easy, go-to way of dealing with negative realities, as it literally allows you to pretend as if something doesn't exist. And while that seems an easy solution in the beginning, it only compounds the problem and makes it more difficult to handle in the future. Trust me, it is much easier to deal with something in the present, as it is happening, than to ignore it and then try to handle it later. Once it gets to that point, it is usually much less manageable than it would have been in the beginning. So if you notice you are adamantly denying something over and over, pay attention to that, as there is probably a reason. Once you've called attention to your denial, you can work to get yourself unstuck and figure out why you are so strongly denying something that at the very least has elements of truth or is completely truthful.

Office Scene: Standing Up for Yourself

The Scene: Stahill Banking

The Problem: A fear of facing the truth

The People: Sandra (a corporate account executive), Samantha (the boss)

Sandra has been working for Stahill Banking as a corporate account executive for five years, and her tenure at the bank has been marked by numerous ups and downs. Although she enjoys what she does, likes the company, and has solid relationships with all of her coworkers, her boss, Samantha, has caused her trouble. Sandra is generally a very positive person, and she likes to think the best about others. So it's been difficult for her the numerous times that her boss has manipulated or taken advantage of her throughout the years. She's often asked to come in on days off to work on important accounts, or to stay late despite any family obligations she may have. In addition to the extra workload she piles on Sandra, Samantha has never been very kind. She's always short with her whenever they speak, and throughout the years she's had very little regard for any personal issues Sandra has encountered. But because Sandra tries to be kind and compassionate she always explains away her boss's behavior, saying that perhaps "Samantha is just having a bad day." Or, "She trusts me more than anyone else; that's why she's always giving me extra work," and "If I want to be the best I can be at my job, I need to be able to handle the extra workload."

It all comes to a head one day when Sandra has to call off work unexpectedly for a funeral. A dear friend of hers has passed away, and Sandra calls Samantha in advance to let her know when she will be absent from work. Although for most a funeral is a perfectly acceptable excuse to miss work, Samantha will have none of it. "I'm sorry about your friend, Sandra, but unfortunately we have a lot to do that day. I'd really appreciate it if you'd come in so that we can meet all of our deadlines."

Dumbfounded, Sandra doesn't quite know how to react. It is the final straw and she refuses to keep denying Samantha's cruelty any longer.

"Listen, Samantha, I have continuously stood by you while others have told me that you're taking advantage of me, that I do way more than you ever acknowledge, and that you really don't care about my feelings or personal life at all. And while I've been denying that for the past five years, it's clear that everyone else around me was correct about what I didn't want to see. And honestly, I'm not going to take it anymore. I am a talented, hard worker, and at this point I would rather take my experience and skills somewhere else than be mistreated and unappreciated here."

"Well, Sandra, that's too bad you feel that way. I thought you could handle a little extra work, but apparently you can't. That's unfortunate," says Samantha nastily.

"No, you're mistaken. It's not the workload that's unmanageable, it's the way you treat people. I'll be coming in later to clean out my things."

And with that Sandra hangs up the phone and feels an immediate release. Once she thinks about it, she realizes she has been making excuses for years because she didn't want to admit the worst. But had she just been honest with herself and taken control of the situation when it began, she would have never had to endure five years of being underappreciated and overworked. Although it is difficult to admit, she feels so much better having taken care of the problem. Although Sandra pledges to remain an optimist, she vows never again to ignore her instinct and go with something that doesn't feel right.

ESTABLISH CLEAR GOALS AND BENCHMARKS

In order to maintain a motivated office community, it's important to continuously communicate its goals and benchmarks. They must be clear, and they must be consistent.

These can be communicated in any number of ways. You could have weekly meetings with your employees, discussing everyone's goals for the week. You could also tell them what you would like accomplished. You could also use a visual, such as a chart that shows how many clients you have gained (and lost), and hang it somewhere in a high-traffic area, such as the break room. Regularly announce and applaud special victories, such as when an employee lands a big client. Alternately, when things are not going as well, be honest with your employees and let them know everyone really needs to pull their weight and put in extra effort.

It's important to establish these measures and bring them up regularly so that your employees know what they're working toward and that growth is important and expected.

Office Scene: Unclear Expectations

The Scene: Matrix Advertising

The Problem: Mixed signals

The People: Christian (an advertising agent), Craig (president)

Christian was recently hired at Matrix Advertising, and he works hard to attract new clients to build his clientele base. Although he finds it a little tough, he still works on his communication with clients and on pitching ideas effectively. Christian is very enthusiastic about his work and thrilled to pursue a career in something about which he is truly passionate. All in all, he is excited about working with new people and growing within the company.

One afternoon his boss, Craig, stops by his office to have a little chat. "Christian," he starts, "I just wanted to have a little talk with you about the rate with which you're bringing in new clients. I know you're still new, but in the past three months that you've been here, you've really only started working, on average, with one client a month. Here at Matrix we expect each of our employees to bring in at least two or three new clients per month. I've appreciated your work and think your advertising concepts are really strong, but I just wanted to have a little talk with you to make sure you're not trying to slack off and that you are actually motivated about your job."

"Oh, wow, Craig. This is really a surprise. I love working here at Matrix, and I'm very excited to start picking up more clients and expanding my clientele base, but no one ever explained to me that there is a client-per-month quota for every employee. Had I known those goals existed, I would have made sure I accomplished them, without a doubt. It's my intention to work to make both myself and Matrix as successful as possible. But for me to be able to do that to my fullest extent, I need to know exactly what your expectations are, as well as the benchmarks for achieving the goals you desire."

"Gosh, Christian, I'm sorry. I didn't realize that I had been so unclear in my communication. You're absolutely right. If I have expectations from my team, I should make sure the entire team knows how I want things done. As well as the consequences for not getting them done."

"Well," Christian suggests, "perhaps we could have a company-wide meeting to formally go over the goals and benchmarks for Matrix so that we're all on the same page. I think that would help me and any other new employees and would be a great refresher for those who've perhaps been letting certain things slide. Or who have plain just forgotten."

Craig agrees that a meeting is a wonderful idea and something that would be helpful and unifying for the entire company. So he calls a meeting later that week and provides each of his employees with a packet, clearly listing and describing his expectations for Matrix and how he wants his employees to go about achieving the goals he's set. Interestingly enough, many of his employees have never been cognizant of some of the goals and therefore hadn't been tailoring their work to achieve the benchmarks Craig thought he had laid out. Once he itemizes them and really specifies the kind of work and overall success he is looking for, his team is appreciative of the information and guidance as to how to better do their jobs.

Through his conversation with Christian, Craig learned that it's of the utmost importance to keep in daily, constant contact with your employees. The only way they're going to know if you want something done is if you tell them. And if it's something as serious as the goals and benchmarks for the company, these should be widely publicized throughout the staff; his weren't.

That has since changed, and things have moved forward drastically for Matrix. Now the employees accomplish things under the same set of guidelines and benchmarks, allowing them to work as a team rather than haphazardly in whatever way they choose. All in all, the staff is motivated, forward moving, and excited about accomplishing the goals that have been laid out for them—a true team.

PAYMENT TRAPS

I believe that no business agreement should feel like a trap, and that if you're not happy with a service you shouldn't be forced to pay for it.

Generally when you hire a PR firm you sign either a six-month or one-year contract. However, these contracts often feel binding and unpleasant for the client, especially if the work isn't as promised.

That's why when Empower PR began I developed a month-by-month payment plan. I strive to keep a very open and authentic relationship with my clients, just as I do with my employees, and it's important to me that our relationship not be constricted by the idea of having a beginning, middle, and end. Rather, as we continue working with our clients, I want those relationships to grow and develop so that we can continue telling their stories as *they* grow and develop.

I believe that my month-by-month payment system provides security to our clients. It also gives security to my company and employees, as we won't have to represent clients who are not happy with our services or who don't fare well under our methods. If this is a concept you are interested in applying in your company, you can do so by first removing any confusing legalese or fine-print loopholes from your contract. Make your contracts as clear and concise as possible, and make your billing system equally simple, with charges laid out in the open for the client to examine. The more authentic your contracts are, the more authentic your relationships and communication will be as a result.

Office Scene: Disappointing Contracts

The Scene: Sharper Channel

The Problem: Unmet expectations

The People: Bob (a publicist), Joshua (the client)

Bob is a publicist at Sharper Channel, a successful PR firm that attracts many important clients and high-profile accounts. A longtime Sharper Channel employee, he has seen his share of difficult clients and difficult situations, but nothing as hard to handle as Blackrock Publishing, the nation's largest bookseller and one of their most reputable accounts.

When the Blackrock Publishing contract starts, Bob feels he is doing a strong job representing the bookseller. He gets their name out into the media right away and is able to work with the company and other sponsors to develop some successful events that garner a lot of publicity and bring a whole host of people into the bookstores.

But after three months, the president of the company, Joshua, calls Bob and tells him that he wants to talk to him about their contract.

"To be honest with you, Bob, we're a little disappointed in how this whole partnership has turned out. We're not pleased with the media you've gotten for us, and we thought that at this point in our contract we'd be represented internationally instead of just nationally. We've been searching around and have talked to a lot of other PR firms who say they could give us a lot more than what you have. So I'm sorry to say it, but I don't think this is going to work out anymore. I've made up my mind, and there's really nothing you can do to change it."

"Joshua, I'm really sorry that you're so disappointed with Sharper Channel, but unfortunately you signed a contract that is binding and unbreakable. It's a one-year contract, and if you do try to break it, we will have to take legal action."

"But this is ridiculous!" Joshua sputters. "If I'm not happy with you and you aren't doing what I want, then why should I have to stay in a contract with you? I am prepared to fight you on this one, because I do not want Blackrock Publishing represented by Sharper Channel any longer. And that's final."

As much as Bob tries to explain to him the situation and what he can do to up their publicity, Joshua will have none of it. He winds up suing the PR firm for "publicity lost during their representation," propelling the two companies into a yearlong legal battle that ends up costing much more than their contract ever would have. In the end, Sharper Channel wins, as they were not in the wrong, but they do lose a lot of time, money, and energy in the legal battle and are very embittered.

After that snafu, Bob has a serious meeting with his CEO, discussing a possible month-by-month payment policy, in case their clients don't like their services or the relationship isn't working out. At first he is worried that they will lose money, but after they institute the policy, they are much happier and they also have happier clients, who trust them strongly.

All in all, it is a strong solution to a very difficult problem. Sharper Channel has stood behind this policy for years now, and it's made them more successful than ever.

- Make your expectations for your employees clear and straightforward.
- Have an easily understood raise/bonus/promotion system that your employees can work toward.
- Make your contracts simple and free of confusing legalese.
- Remember, if you spot it, you got it—so if you find that you intensely dislike someone or something, it might be because you have that very same trait hidden within you!

TESTIMONIALS

B y now you no doubt are wondering what it is like to work in a No-Gossip Zone and authentic work environment! It certainly is quite a bit different. Here my employees tell in their own words what it is like to work and live authentically:

MICHELLE MEKKY—PRESIDENT

My previous career before coming to Empower PR was in the media. I spent twelve years working at a television station as a writer and, eventually, senior producer. I would say I probably heard gossip, or gossiped about someone, just about every day. And I am not talking only about Britney Spears's latest crisis or Jessica Simpson's newest boyfriend. It was very common for employees to gossip about each other, the bosses, and anyone else we could find to talk about! I just thought it was completely normal to have this type of work atmosphere. I had my buddies I would gab with every day, in between producing live shows, writing scripts, and booking segments.

But when I later made a career change and decided to come to Empower PR, I had no idea just how different the work atmosphere would be.

I knew that Sam was learning all of these really innovative and different workplace practices from his life coach. He would come in my office after a session and start dropping all of these nuggets he learned. Soon our conversations became about new concepts to me, like triangle games, personas, shifting, and, of course, the No-Gossip Zone. I barely understood what he was talking about, so finally I started seeing the life coach so I could learn his language.

And when the No-Gossip Zone concept was introduced to me, part of me thought it was nuts. I mean, how can you exist without gossip? And furthermore, as a manager at the company, does that mean I can't talk about my employees? But I quickly learned how it all works and how to stop it when it happens. At first anytime someone would come to me and say something I thought was gossip, I would become extremely nervous. But eventually I got used to stopping gossip as it was happening and telling the person gossiping they had to go complete with the one they were talking about or I would. They would get a look of horror on their face. And gradually the gossip ended! It was truly amazing. A few times I was the one who had to do the completing, and I was so horrified from that experience it was enough to make me not want to gossip ever again. I have made people cry, and I have cried. But once

I got through those awkward, scary moments, the No-Gossip Zone became a lighter, happier way to live at work. I feel like a burden has been lifted in a lot of ways.

Persona play has truly changed my life as well, both inside and outside of the office. Who knew I had so many personalities? Before I truly understood what a persona is, in the middle of a conversation Sam would say to me, "What persona am I talking to right now?" And I thought to myself: I have no idea! I would feel angry at times because I became confused and didn't really know how to communicate. So it definitely took some work for me to understand the inner workings of my personas and how they affect my day-to-day life. I really started to understand it when we were at our first life coach retreat with the team in Michigan. Our coach asked us to name some of our personas. Then she asked for volunteers to stand up and act some of them out in a very exaggerated way. No one was volunteering, and since part of me has always wanted to be on the stage, I jumped up and said, "I'll play out 'Polly the Pleaser'." I proceeded to demonstrate how I just wanted everyone to like me, and the room roared with laughter. And at that very moment I realized just how strong this desire to please everyone exists in me. But at the same time, it's completely draining me!

I also learned that I have a "Wanda the Worrier" persona, a "Sally the Superwoman" persona, and the "I wish I were a star" persona as well. I can't explain all of them, but I know it changes minute to minute, so you never know what you are going to get! But learning what a persona is, and how I fall into the traps of my personas, helps me to find my true self and just exist in ease and flow, which is really where I am always striving to be.

KATE STREIT—PUBLICIST

My experience working at Empower PR has been unique, starting with my interview. I was very nervous, and I came in trying to recite what I thought would be important answers in my head. *Who are my favorite columnists and why? What are my three biggest strengths and weaknesses?* My prospective employer caught me off guard, though, and asked me questions that were more about me as a person than me as an employee, at least what I had come to think of as the definition of an employee. It was clear that hard skills like knowledge of a certain database program, for example, were less important than character strengths like honesty and enthusiasm for your work.

I have worked in both a large corporate environment and a small family business, both of which had their good and bad points, but coming to Empower PR was a definite positive change. I felt very replaceable and not at all valued as a person in the corporate environment. A lot of the policies in place here let me know that my time and work are important. For example, we are allowed to leave the office early when we come in early in the morning for a TV segment. In my corporate position I didn't feel that my time was respected in this way. I sometimes had to stay late and was never thanked or compensated for my extra work and time in any way.

At the family business my boss knew and respected me as a person, but also did not have respect for my time or boundaries. I would often receive late-night, early morning, or weekend phone calls and emails, and I felt obligated to respond. The anxiety of never being able to really be away from work wore on me, and I began to resent my job. Being able to have time to myself when I don't have to worry about work is essential for me to be as rested and productive as possible when I *am* at work.

The policies at Empower PR are designed to value the employee, and I think they produce the best results. A happy employee is a hardworking and great employee!

AMANDA ALDINGER—WRITER

After reading the copious news coverage about Sam's philosophy of the No-Gossip Zone, as well as his various theories on authentic communication in the workplace, I was interested to become Empower PR's newest hire to see how his theories were actually implemented at the office. Now, granted, I've only been working with Empower PR for a week, but I can firmly attest to the quality of the work environment and the communicative openness of its employees without fail.

As someone who comes solely from an arts background, launching myself into an urban Chicago PR firm was pretty outside the bounds of any prior work experience I'd had to date, and I wasn't quite sure what to expect. Add to that an office completely comprised of women (save one lovely gentleman) and you've got a newbie wondering if she's going to be eaten alive.

But then the day progressed. It began in the kitchen, where we all read the papers, discussed the news, and caffeinated for the day. Everyone was so kind in helping to get me set up, showing me where everything was located, and in helping to make my transition as "new girl" as painless as possible. As the day went on and I observed my surroundings, I quickly realized that Sam really had been successful in creating a work environment where everyone communicated and everyone owned their 100% of making Empower PR a successful public relations firm.

I've worked my fair share of jobs where my best interests, emotionally and professionally, were not my employer's primary interest. But at Empower PR it's made very clear—with policies such as "no BlackBerrys or work emails past six or on the weekends" and a catered, communal hour lunch every day of the week—that a happy work/life balance truly is important. Our management staff knows that if we, as their employees, aren't happy and don't feel as if our contributions are being respected, we aren't going to believe in the company, and we're not going to be motivated to come to work every day to do our jobs. And because of that, they work hard to make sure they communicate authentically with us, just as we're expected to respond authentically and own our 100% when it comes to our job responsibilities.

I already feel that this is the most positive work environment I've ever been in, and it's great to be a part of something that defies typical office politics and woes. The No-Gossip Zone is the zone for me!

ANDREA CORDTS—SENIOR PUBLICIST

About a few months after I began working at Empower PR, I was informed that we would be having a group life coach session. Now, I had never even heard of a life coach before my time at Empower PR, so I was quite confused about what this meant.

During my short time in corporate America, I have learned a few things the hard way— the first being that the "higher ups" don't care what you think or how you feel. I was reprimanded at my previous job for answering the company president's inquiry about one of my accounts truthfully rather than responding with a sugary "everything's great, thank you!" My direct supervisor explained as nicely as she could that this was how it works. Unfortunately, it took another incident for me to actually get the point.

So you can imagine my surprise when the CEO of Empower PR sat down in the circle with us, urging us to share our feelings and completions, even if they had to do with him. He said it was okay to cry or get angry, because that's how you move your emotions. I couldn't believe it!

That day I learned a lot about my coworkers, bosses, and the company atmosphere as a whole. There was some hesitation about "completing" with people, but in the end there were a lot of things being said that weren't being communicated before. People did cry. People did get angry. And at the urging of the life coach moderating the experience, several conflicts were resolved.

The most interesting aspect of the session, however, was that it didn't end when we filed out of the room at five o'clock. Those who did not feel comfortable speaking in a large group sought each other out to either discuss problems they may have been having or to appreciate each other's work.

To be completely honest, I didn't participate in the session. I sat and listened to what was going on, but I was still new to the company, and I was waiting to be told yet again that my honesty had gotten me in trouble. Fortunately, that has changed. As I become more comfortable with my surroundings and company atmosphere, I am able to utilize the tools I learned in the life coach session to communicate my *true* thoughts and feelings to others within the company.

Working in a company full of women is not always easy, but by communicating effectively with each other, we have been able to make it work and thrive in the process.

LIFE COACHES

My first introduction to the philosophies in this book came courtesy of my affiliation with the Young Presidents Organization. The Young Presidents Organization is a group of twelve presidents who gather to support, encourage, and assist one another as businesspeople and as individuals. As part of the annual Young Presidents Organization forum, I discovered life coach Diana Chapman, who shared many new theories that helped me to become a better communicator and a better manager.

When I shared these theories with my colleagues and some of my employees, I realized how beneficial and life-changing these new communication techniques could be. That's when I decided to make over my entire office into a place of authentic communication, a place where gossip was banned and emotional honesty was a must. It was a risk, and certainly not one that other corporate, white-collar bosses would have taken. But I saw the power and impor-tance of these new ideas, and despite some small resistance,

I saw how willing my staff was to become a part of this new corporate world.

Since meeting with my first life coach, my life has never been the same, which is why I encourage every manager and every employee to try a life coach meeting at least once.

Here is a list of some of the best life coaches in the business:

Diana Chapman is a transformational coach who is inherently and totally for you, sees your magic and your power, and calls you to it in the most playful, loving ways imaginable. She specializes in working with corporate and political leaders, supporting their relationships at work and at home and with themselves. She is the combination of a masterful seer, a revolutionary lover, and a world-class leader. She leads you into the territory of yourself where your real power resides. She shows you how to take the sword out of the stone, and you become king and wizard of your reality.

Contact Diana

If you would like to schedule an appointment or learn more, please call or email Monday through Friday, 8:00 a.m. to 5:00 p.m.

831-476-4840 (PST)

Email: diana@dianachapman.com

Jack Skeen has been studying and working in the area of human potential and coaching for the past thirty-five years. He has served as mentor and coach for many CEOs and senior executives of Fortune 500 companies.

Jack is exceptionally talented at identifying obstacles that create a "ceiling effect" to success for individuals, relationships, and teams. He is skilled at communicating what people need to know but often seek to overlook, in ways that make the information highly useful.

Before entering the world of coaching, Jack founded a private psychotherapy practice, where he worked for ten years. He holds advanced degrees in theology from Westminster Theological Seminary and a PhD in psychology from Biola University.

Jim Dethmer is a world-class coach, speaker, and team builder. He has lectured before more than 250,000 people worldwide. Jim has worked with teams and executives from leading investment organizations, domestically and internationally, strengthening their effectiveness through customized coaching and consulting interventions. His keen insights and straightforward delivery of powerful and practical principles enable individuals, teams, and organizations to achieve breakthrough results in personal growth and profitability.

Additionally, Jim has been featured on webcasts for the CFA Institute, covering the topics of world-class decision making and the essential behaviors of high-performing investment teams. Jim is coauthor of *High Performing Investment Teams* (Wiley, 2006) and is a graduate of Texas Christian University with a BS in business management.

Contact Jack and Jim

Focus Consulting Group, Inc.

4137 Three Lakes Drive

Long Grove, Illinois 60047

Jack Skeen: 410-785-7145

For general inquiries, please call: 847-853-8251

Email: info@focuscgroup.com

http://focuscgroup.com

Christine Godwin is a certified life and relationship coach who has studied with some of the greatest teachers of our time. She studied for four years with renowned relationship experts and best selling authors Drs. Gay and Kathlyn Hendricks and graduated from their apprentice program. Christine has attended lectures and workshops given by Deepak Chopra, Marianne Williamson, Gangagi, Eli Jaxon-Bear, Patch Adams, Jean Huston, Wayne Dyer, and many others.

Christine has been on a quest for most of her life to understand the nature of being. Having endured an abusive first marriage, she set out to learn everything she could about how to create peace in her life and in the world. Her work as a life coach and inspirational speaker seeks to heal those who choose to improve their lives.

Contact Christine
Phone: 805-272-5242
E-mail: info@ChristineGodwin.com
http://www.christinegodwin.com

Jim Warner is a dedicated coach, guide, and facilitator to senior executives, guiding them into candid, creative, and collaborative interactions for enhanced performance at both the enterprise and whole-life levels. Having worked with more than 1,500 CEOs; countless executive teams from fast-growth, high-performance companies; and dozens of couples navigating difficult midlife transitions, Jim is a recognized expert at helping individuals, couples, and teams achieve greater self-awareness; authentic, productive communication; more fulfilling relationships—and more satisfying lives.

Contact Jim
Phone: 303-449-7770; 303-817-8100 (cell)
Email: req1@oncourseinternational.com
http://www.oncourseinternational.com/about/jwarner.htm

ABOUT THE AUTHOR

Samuel P. Chapman is chief executive officer of Empower Public Relations, Chicago's most accomplished new PR firm, with its focus on television appearances. Empower has clients in a variety of industries, ranging from the nation's leading sex therapist, Space Command's "Stress Doctor," and to ultra-premium liquor brands. Every Empower client has one crucial thing in common—they are good on television.

Chapman is chairman of the board of Berman Health and Media, Inc., a public company he started to produce television, radio, and print media in the area of women's sexual health. In that role he also served as the executive producer of *Sexual Healing* on Showtime Networks. *Sexual Healing* is a nine-episode documentary series starring his wife, Dr. Laura Berman. The show follows Dr. Berman as she treats three couples per show for their sexual problems.

The company also runs a couples therapy clinic and has its own products, DVD series, and a subscription website: www.drlauraberman.com.

Before founding Empower Public Relations, Chapman was president of a venture capital company named Parson Capital. He also founded a consulting firm named Parson Group, which in 2000 achieved *Inc.* magazine's top rating as the fastest-growing company in the nation (number one on "The Inc. 500"). The company was sold to a British public company for $55 million in cash.

Chapman's knowledge and passion for public relations inspired him to open Empower Public Relations in 2006. With extensive expertise in television production, he knows what producers need for great segments. His far-reaching, individualized client campaigns focus on shared experiences, resulting in hundreds of millions of media impressions every year.

Chapman is a member of the Young Presidents Organization (YPO) and of the Economic Club of Chicago.